Armonia
Casilla 3081
Santa Cruz de la Sierra
Bolivia

Kookaburras

Great Brown Kingfisher (more commonly called the Laughing Kookaburra) drawn by John White, Surgeon General to the first fleet and the settlement at Port Jackson. This drawing is taken from his Journal of a Voyage to New South Wales, *published in 1790.*

Kookaburras

Veronica A. Parry

TAPLINGER PUBLISHING COMPANY
NEW YORK

First published in the United States in 1972 by
TAPLINGER PUBLISHING CO., INC.
New York, New York
Copyright © 1970 by Veronica Parry
All rights reserved.
Printed in Hong Kong
No part of this publication may be reproduced or transmitted
in any form or by any means, electronic or mechanical,
including photocopy, recording, or any information storage
and retrieval system now known or to be invented, except by
a reviewer who wishes to quote brief passages in connection
with a review written for inclusion in a magazine, newspaper
or broadcast.
Published simultaneously in the Dominion of Canada by
Burns & MacEachern Ltd., Ontario
Library of Congress Catalog Card Number: 71-183133
ISBN 0-8008-4490-4

To Ernie
in memory of our days
on The Hill

CONTENTS

    Preface   9
1. Introducing *Dacelo gigas*   11
    Some History and Zoogeography   12
2. Plumage Characters and Age Classes   17
3. The Kookaburra's Social System   22
4. The Size and Function of Territory   34
5. Vocal Behaviour   42
    The Laugh Song   42
    The Calls   47
6. Visual Behaviour   54
    General Behaviour   54
    Courtship Behaviour   63
    Territorial Defence Behaviour   66
7. Breeding Biology   78
    Nests, Eggs and Incubation   80
    The Chicks and Fledglings   84
8. Mortality and Predation   96
9. Why Have Auxiliaries?   98
    List of Scientific Names   107
    Bibliography   109

Great Brown Kings Fisher.

PREFACE

The kookaburra is wholly an Australian bird, but many people throughout the world have had the pleasure of watching it and listening to its peculiar laugh, for almost every major zoo exhibits at least one pair of kookaburras along with other examples of Australia's unique wildlife.

It so happened that I met my first pair of kookaburras in the San Diego Zoo while I worked there part-time to put myself through university. My fascination for this bird can only be expressed by the fact that I honestly used to go to work early just to sit in front of its cage and wait for it to laugh. While sitting there on those crisp, clear mornings I used to think how wonderful it would be if only I could go to Australia and study the kookaburra in its natural setting. Two years later, the dream became a reality; Professor Marshall of Monash University offered me a postgraduate scholarship and within a week I was on a boat heading for the great Antipodes.

For the next two years my husband and I lived in the Dandenong Ranges near Belgrave, Victoria, where we devoted our time to finding out everything there was to know about this friendly yet mysterious bird. The end result of this research was the granting of a Master of Science degree and then the opportunity to write this book.

The gathering of data however, was certainly not accomplished single-handed. My husband, Ernie, took a year off from his own career to help establish the field routine. Then my mother, Mrs Kay Preston, came to visit Australia and inadvertently became a very helpful field assistant.

The people on Terry's Hill, Belgrave, not only opened their gates and hearts to me in a typical Australian fashion, but were most helpful in personally gathering valuable information on their back-yard birds. Without their help, the task of piecing the puzzle together would have been much more difficult. Foremost among these fine people were Mr and Mrs Wm. Hale who not only introduced us to Belgrave's kookaburras, but spent many hours in the field watching and recording whenever special help was needed. To their devotion and friendship, I am deeply indebted.

There is an embarrassingly long list of academic colleagues who helped me make the kookaburra's story a valuable piece of scientific research. These people have been acknowledged in the scientific publication of this work, but I do want to thank again my patient supervisor, Dr Doug Dorward.

Robert Hardie, Carol and Ian Bevege gave their careful scrutiny to this manuscript and I thank them for their suggestions and encouragement.

And last but not least, I wish to thank Aunt Clara and all her friends for putting up with the indignities of being trapped and tagged, and for allowing me to poke my binoculars into their private lives. To these patient and forbearing kookaburras, both the author and those who read this book are most grateful.

Veronica A. Parry, BA., MSc.

1. INTRODUCING DACELO GIGAS

An Aboriginal legend tells us that Agoodenout, the keeper of the sun's fire, sent the kookaburra to awaken man and all the bushland creatures to the glories of a new day. For centuries between the origin of this legend and the present, Australians have been listening to the laughter of the kookaburra and still have not found a better explanation for it.

A journey through folklore shows that as in this legend, men have always had a somewhat personal relationship with the kookaburra. The bird may laugh along with man in a merry mood or it may laugh mockingly at man's folly. Some say that it laughs to warn man of forthcoming rain or even danger. Only recently, it was suggested that the kookaburra can afford to have a mirthful chuckle at us, for in spite of centuries of folklore his intimate secrets have been known only to him.

If this is true, we can now smile quietly in reply, for at last we can share in the private joke. The kookaburra's way of life is no longer a mystery and we even know with certainty why he laughs. But there is more to this bird than the simple tale of its life cycle. Having unlocked those intimate secrets, we made the uncanny discovery that man and kookaburra have much more in common than the familiar guffaw. In adapting to the Australian environment, this aberrant kingfisher has evolved a social structure and a territorial system very similar and in some ways identical to our own.

Most of us enjoy reading about animals that are like us in one way or another and for that reason alone the kookaburra's story is an intriguing one. To the biologist, however, the study of social and territorial behaviour has just recently come to the fore and is receiving some long overdue attention, especially in the light of man's overpopulation problems. Could social and territorial behaviour have evolved as a method of controlling the number of individuals in a population?

The most direct way to answer this big question is to turn to those animals who employ these systems as part of their way of life and to try and glean the facts from them. Two years of living with kookaburras have shown us that their social and territorial behaviour may well curb their numbers and thus control their population. Although we need more data on the subject, it isn't bad progress considering that it took centuries to find out simply why a kookaburra laughs.

Some History and Zoogeography

The kookaburra's ancestors, members of the genus *Dacelo*, come from New Guinea. The two Australian species of this genus are *D. leachii*, the northern Blue-winged Kookaburra and *D. gigas*, the southern Great Brown Kingfisher, more commonly called the Laughing Kookaburra. There is a subspecies of the Laughing Kookaburra called *D. gigas minor*, so named because although very similar to its relative, it is a much smaller bird. From the map on page 19 we see that *D. leachii* occupies the hotter more northern latitudes of the continent reaching as far down as Brisbane where it is only an occasional visitor. *D. gigas* prefers the cooler, wetter parts of Australia's east coast, but overlaps with *D. leachii* by occasionally extending up as far north as Cape York. *D. gigas minor* is found on the far northern tip of Cape York and extends only down to the Jardine River. It is probably able to maintain its sub-specific characters because it is completely isolated from *D. gigas*.

Oddly enough, the kookaburra is not naturally found in Tasmania or Western Australia. The birds were transported there by man around 1900 and they have flourished ever since. Could their absence in Western Australia and Tasmania possibly mean that kookaburras evolved after desert and water cut these places off from eastern Australia? If so, kookaburras are very recent birds indeed. The species was also introduced to New Zealand around the 1900's but failed to become established.

The first white man to become acquainted with the kookaburra must have been aboard the *Endeavour* on Captain Cook's voyage between 1769 and 1771 for two specimens were found among Sir Joseph Banks' collection. However, no records or notes were made on the bird or its peculiar laugh.[2]*

The first written word we find about the kookaburra comes from Pierre Sonnerat in his *Voyage to New Guinea*, published in Paris in 1776. He states, 'The two Kingfishers which I observed at New Guinea are much larger than the largest species of this genus hitherto known.'[21] He then proceeds to describe the bird and includes an excellent drawing opposite. From this, it is indisputable that he is referring to the Great Brown Kingfisher, yet our eyebrows are raised in question since the bird does not occur in New Guinea. It also seems odd that Sonnerat should elaborately describe the bird's plumage without mentioning its raucous laughter which, as a naturalist living on the land, he surely should have noticed. Two explanations have been proposed to solve

* See Bibliography

Pierre Sonnerat's kookaburra, the first drawing ever made of this bird, taken from his Voyage a la Nouvelle Guinée *published in 1776.*

this mystery. Alexander[2] brings to our attention the fact that most of the birds which Sonnerat drew and described were either skins purchased from the natives or were tame birds kept as pets. It is just possible that native fishermen hunting the trepang and mother of pearl down the Australian coast may have secured the two kookaburras to keep as pets or for barter since birds were highly-valued items of trade and that Sonnerat drew and described these captives.

There is, however, another argument as to how Sonnerat could have led us to believe that the kookaburra was indigenous to New Guinea. Lysaght uncovered an old letter written by Sonnerat to Banks which may reveal a bit of skull-duggery. Sonnerat met Banks at the Cape of Gook Hope in 1770 and in this letter he thanks Banks for giving him some of the new birds which Banks found in his travels. Thus, it is possible that Sonnerat described skins actually collected by Banks or Solander and cheated by stating he observed them in New Guinea. Lysaght points out that Sonnerat did not have many scruples when it came to using other people's material. For instance, he published plates of southern penguins and said they were a New Guinea species when in fact they were drawn by a man named Jossigny from a collection made by Cammerson on his voyage around the world from 1766 to 1769.[10]

Perhaps we will never know the true story behind the first observation of the kookaburra but whether by error or intent, it will soon be seen that Sonnerat's ghost still lurks around our wholly Australian bird.

Museum taxonomists did not pay much attention to animal collections from the Antipodes until 1783, at which time the kookaburra was the second Australian bird to receive a scientific name.[9] Boddaert called it *Alcedo gigas*. However another taxonomist, Hermann, read Sonnerat's book and gave the bird what he thought to be the more appropriate name of *Dacelo novaguineae*. Unfortunately, he published this name just fifteen days before Boddaert.[11] In 1923, members of the twenty-first R.A.O.U. Congress attempted to straighten things out by combining the name into *Dacelo gigas*[14] and it still stands as such in the *Official Checklist of the Birds of Australia*.[13] Unfortunately, Mr Sonnerat's mischief lingers on because the name *gigas* is invalid by priority so *Dacelo novaguineae* is the only legal name and though misleading it is being adopted in the new checklist which is currently being revised.

The name *Dacelo* is an anagram of *Alcedo* from *halcyon*, the kingfishers' classic name given them by the Greeks. A myth tells how Alcyone, daughter of the god of the winds, plunged into the sea to join her drowned husband and Zeus, to spare them, turned them into kingfishers. The ancient Greeks thought that kingfishers built floating nests far out at sea and bred in early December, so the myth goes on to say that every year the gods calmed the waters for these birds so they could breed successfully. Ever since then calm winter days are referred to as halcyon days. The kookaburras present specific name, *gigas*, is

The author with a young kookaburra.

Latin for big, not laughing as some may think.

How the kookaburra came by its vernacular name, the Laughing Jackass is and will probably always be a mystery. From the writings of Thomas Walting, we know this name was in vogue in New South Wales between 1788 and 1792[1] but we must progress to 1801 to find the first nature note on the bird and its peculiar laugh. George Caley, an explorer and naturalist, was sent to Australia by Banks in 1800 and while on a collecting trip around Jervis Bay he 'saw the Laughing Bird, so called from the noise it makes resembling laughter'.[4]

In 1802, Caley began collecting birds and elaborated further on the kookaburra. 'The settlers call this bird the *Laughing Jackass* and the natives, as I think, *Cuck'unda*. It is common throughout the colony, at least in all the forest land of the interior parts. It makes a loud noise somewhat like laughing which may be heard at a considerable distance, from which circumstance, and its uncouth appearance, it probably received the above extraordinary appellation from the settlers on their first arrival in the colony. I have also heard it called the Hawkesbury Clock (clocks being at the period of my residence scarce articles in the colony, there not being one perhaps in the whole Hawkesbury settlement) for it is amongst the first of the feathered tribe which announces the approach of day. When sleeping in the woods I have often found its singular voice most welcome in the morning.'[4]

Since this first note, many a pen has scratched both humorous and woeful anecdotes about the Laughing Jackass. For example, C. H. Eden wrote in 1872, 'At daylight came a hideous chorus of fiendish laughter, as if the infernal regions had been broken loose—this was the song of another feathered innocent, the laughing jackass—not half a bad sort of fellow when you come to know him, for he kills snakes, and is an infallible sign of the vicinity of fresh-water.'[12]

From his book *Victoria in 1880*, Garnet Walsh takes a more unkindly view of our kookaburra. 'Dense forests, where the prolonged cachinnations of that cynic of the woods, as A. P. Maring calls the laughing jackass, seemed to mock us for our pains.'[12]

On a lighter note, C. Lumholtz in 1890 said 'Few of the birds of Australia have pleased me as much as this curious laughing jackass, though it is both clumsy and unattractive in colour. Far from deserving its name jackass, it is on the contrary very wise and also very courageous. It boldly attacks venomous snakes and large lizards, and is consequently the friend of the colonist.'[12] It is fortunate for our clumsy curious friend that most of us today still share Mr Lumholtz's view.

2. PLUMAGE CHARACTERS AND AGE CLASSES

Besides being a handy guide in field identification, the study of plumage can tell us a lot about a bird's biology. Often fledglings, juveniles and adult birds acquire a characteristic plumage with each moult so that the age and often the sex of many birds can be told simply by their plumage. Blue Wrens, for instance, are good examples of this.

In some species too, adult males and females may be readily distinguished from one another on the basis of plumage differences, referred to as dichromatism. On the other hand, if two kookaburras are seen side by side, it would be difficult to tell which was male and which was female because their overall plumages are very similar. Why is it then that in some species, dichromatism is evident and in others it is not? The answer is that colour, like voice, is a form of communication. Usually species with dichromatic characters are solitary (i.e. not social) and are not permanently mated. In some solitary birds such as some ducks and many songbirds where the male must find a new mate every year, it is advantageous that he possess a brightly coloured plumage as well as a good voice to court a prospective mate. The female, being the chooser, need not look attractive and so remains drab. This drabness is advantageous as protective colouration when she is incubating eggs in the open. To these non-social birds, the difference in plumage marks the difference between sexes, and when two birds of the same species meet, their reaction to one another is largely determined by the difference or similarity in colour. So, during the breeding season a male will fight another brightly coloured bird, this aggressive behaviour being triggered by the distinctive colour pattern, but when faced by a drab coloured bird, he will begin courting behaviour.

In terms of vocal and visual communication, it is likely that once courtship is over, there is very little to be said between a solitary pair. The essentials are carried out vocally and a difference in dress does not complicate the communication system. If, however, we consider a social species in which information must be conveyed to a number of individuals all year round, we can see that if all individuals had a different plumage and vocal dialect, communication would indeed be complicated and disadvantageous. As with the military system, the most efficient means of mass communication is for all members to dress alike and use a uniform terminology which is not likely to be confused. And so it is for most social species of birds. Male and female either tell each other apart by certain behavioural postures or are permanently mated. Where all males and females look alike, several adult males can coexist in the same family for there is no stimulus to trigger aggression during the breeding season.

It is probably for these reasons that there are few or no plumage or vocal differences between age groups or sexes in kookaburras. The chicks, which are naked when hatched, develop directly into adult plumage. For the first three months of their fledgling life, however, their age can be told, for even though they are the same general size of the adults, they have a very short tail and beak. The mandible or jaw of the bill remains black, gradually turning to a bone colour as the three months lapse. There are other slight differences in fledglings which are helpful in field identification. The plumage tends to be darker than that of adults simply because it is new. Gradual wear soon causes it to lighten to the normal colour within six months. Often the white band on the tip of the tail is very broad but this too becomes narrow as the feathers wear.

A juvenile kookaburra is between three and twelve months old. This is a difficult age class to identify in the field because although no moult has taken place in the transition from fledgling to juvenile, growth and wear of the plumage render it very similar in all respects to the adult. To tell juveniles from adults we must rely on behavioural differences. These are easily detected, especially during the breeding season.

A juvenile enters adulthood at the age of twelve months, for at this time it is sexually mature and capable of breeding. But as kookaburras moult only once a year after the breeding season, there is a span of fourteen months before a juvenile moults and replaces the plumage it acquired in the nest. This first moult is called the post-juvenile moult and in most species marks the beginning of adulthood. Because of this, there may be a bit of confusion in separating juveniles from adults during this nebulous period of two months between breeding and moulting. The best solution is to say that a bird is adult if it breeds, even though it may be doing so in juvenile plumage.

Adult plumage patterns are interesting for in this age class we see a vestigial remnant of what once may have been a dichromatic character. Although in the majority of cases the two sexes are identical, sometimes a male develops a bright blue rump. On close examination of the two sexes, females sometimes have a slight blue tinge imposed on the normal brown colour of the rump but in no case have they been known to have a bright blue rump like some males.

An interesting observation sheds some light on the function of this plumage

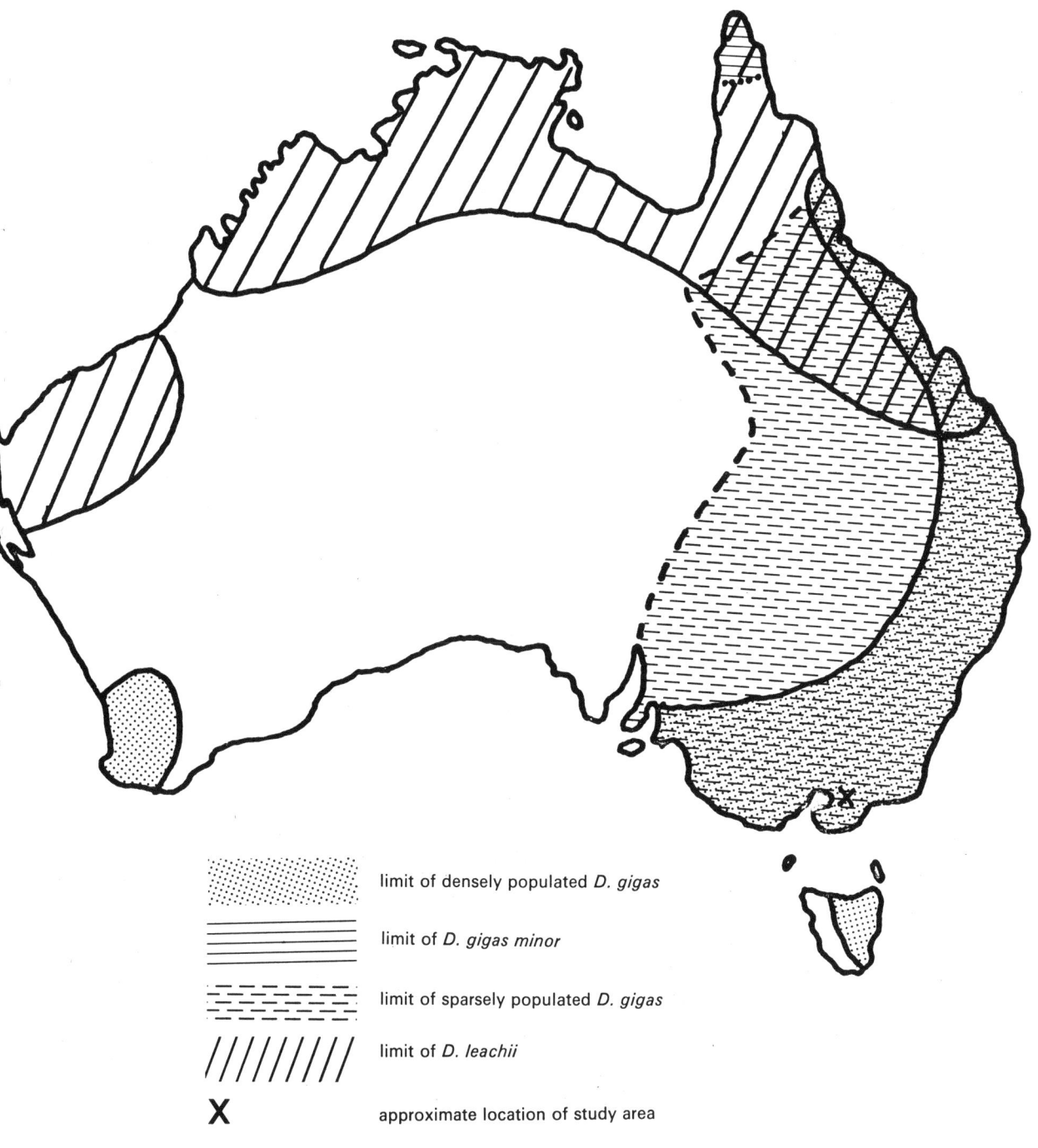

Map showing distribution of kookaburras in Australia.

difference between the sexes. After the above statement, you can imagine my surprise when I walked into the territory of a bright-rumped widowed male and found him courting an equally bright-rumped bird. I was about to throw my brilliant theory out the window but stopped long enough to notice a sequence of very peculiar behaviour. The widowed male would pass food to his blue-rumped bride, a typical event called courtship feeding. She responded in a feminine way of soft squawks and total submission. Then he would fly to a certain scar in a tree near his boundary and perform a trapeze display. This, as we will see, is a territorial defence behaviour, an act designed to evict an outsider. In essence, this widowed male was both courting and fighting with his prospective mate. This behaviour continued for several days with a fervour yet unmatched by any amorous kookaburra. Obviously both the widowed male and I had doubts about this new-comer. Neither of us had heard of a blue-rumped female. So I trapped this bird and performed a harmless operation; a tiny slit into the side of the etherised bird to look at its gonads. Sure enough, 'she' was male! After a stitch in the side, the bird awoke and returned to its role of the great imposter. Apparently our widowed male was about to make the same discovery himself, for the very next day he chased 'her' out of his territory and within two days was seen truly courting a plain brown-rumped female who eventually proved her sex beyond all doubt by laying three eggs.

What all this means is that blue-rumped birds are always male and other males, like our widower, respond to this. However, since not all males have blue rumps, behaviour is the main distinguisher of sex. Our widower was responding to two stimuli: submissive behaviour elicited courtship while the blue rump elicited aggression. This, of course, resulted in the ambivalent behaviour observed. Since then I have seen the initial stage of courtship between an older male and a prospective mate. Though she was brown-rumped, as are many males, it was her complete submission and low feminine squawks which served as the key to her admission into the male's territory. This is another indication that in the main, behaviour indicates the sex of the individual.

Albinos and semi-albino kookaburras occur in about five per cent of the population. They are known to mate with normal birds, once again indicating that plumage is not important in sex recognition. Since behaviour has taken over this role, and most males are now brown-rumped, the dichromatism observed is probably disappearing from the population. Since it no longer has adaptive value, we may regard it as a vestige from the days when it did function as an indicator of the sex of the individual.

True Albino Kookaburra found in Gippsland, Victoria in 1928. (Fleay)

3. THE KOOKABURRA'S SOCIAL SYSTEM

The two most popular questions asked about kookaburras are whether or not they live in the same area year round and why they tend to congregate in groups of three or more individuals. Until this study no one knew the answer to either question. But both mysteries were solved once we developed a system of identifying individual birds by attaching a brightly coloured tag to the wing. So tagged, it was not long before the birds themselves demonstrated their answers for us. To the first query we were soon shown that kookaburras were indeed territorial and that they occupied the same territory year round. As we shall see in the next chapter, they also showed us how these territories were of prime importance to their whole way of life.

But the answer to the second query, why they tend to congregate in groups of three or more individuals, was not apparent at first. We started tagging in the non-breeding season and found that in some territories, in addition to the permanently-mated pair, there were other kookaburras also in residence. We first thought that these were juveniles from the previous year's breeding season who would leave the territory when the parents bred again. After all, that is the normal procedure for many species of birds. But we were surprised to find that when egg-laying started these birds didn't leave, but actually shared in the nesting duties by incubating eggs, feeding and protecting chicks and fledglings along with the parents. In some cases there were up to four helpers all carrying out nesting duties as arduously as if the young were their own. This is an uncommon type of cooperation in the animal kingdom, one which we tend to associate with higher primates and man. It was certainly the last thing we expected to find in our Australian kookaburra.

Because this social system is such a basic part of this bird's way of life, it is worthwhile looking at a few family histories in detail and retracing the steps that ultimately led us to a full understanding of it.

In one territory there were three birds. The mated pair were obvious from their courtship behaviour but the third bird really puzzled us, for she was persistent in helping with nesting duties, and yet had no mate and was never

Tagging birds for study purposes.

seen in courtship with the only male of the territory. For lack of another name, we called her Aunt Clara. The name 'aunt' soon turned out to be inappropriate for we found that in other territories, the odd members playing this auxiliary role were males. So the name 'auxiliary' was given to these helpers.

Our next problem was to find what their relationship to the mated pair was and what determined the number of auxiliaries in any one territory. First, we tagged the chicks from the 1965 breeding season. In Aunt Clara's group, two of the three fledglings survived and stayed within their parents' territory. From the time they left the nest they began to defend the territory along with Aunt Clara and the parents. It appeared then that Aunt Clara was the daughter of the mating pair. When the 1966 breeding season rolled around, none of the family left. Again the pair engaged in courtship and began egg-laying. Then, to our utter fascination, the two juveniles from 1965 started to help, sharing in the incubation of eggs and feeding of young along with Aunt Clara and her parents. In this case, five birds helped to rear the brood. This pattern was repeated in other territories. Where the young from the previous season survived, they stayed and functioned as auxiliaries.

In both years roughly half of the territories we studied had auxiliaries. By watching the changes that occurred we saw that former auxiliary groups could be reduced to solitary pairs. For example, one territory in 1965 had two male auxiliaries and the pair. These four birds raised two chicks, but before the year was out disaster struck; some youngsters decided to use the kookaburras for target practice, and within a week we found two birds dead from bullet wounds. Two other members disappeared and may have succumbed to the same fate. This left only two birds in the group, the breeding male and female. The female was so badly wounded that her mate had to hunt for food and feed her continuously. Her wound never healed and though permanently disabled and dependent on her mate for survival, she attempted to breed the next season and managed to lay one egg before she died from her four-month-old injury.

In another territory there resided three birds, the mated pair and an auxiliary called Big Red after the colour of her tag. Like Aunt Clara, she appeared adult when we first met her in 1965 and she helped rear her parents offspring in 1966. In an attempt to understand this auxiliary system better, we trapped and removed the breeding female from the territory which, by the way, was right next door to Aunt Clara's territory. Now, would Big Red mate with her widowed father or would he choose someone from outside? The time was August, one month before breeding began, so a decision was near at hand.

Late one afternoon Aunt Clara was missing from her territory and early next morning I almost dropped my binoculars with the utter shock of seeing Aunt Clara with the next door widower! The pair bond between these two became firmly cemented that day and oddly enough, Big Red seemed to accept

These photographs show the best method of trapping birds for tagging.

the situation. Unfortunately things soon became confused. A new pair was seeking a territory at this time and with the widowed male more intent on courting than defending, this new pair obtained a toehold into a portion of his territory. Aunt Clara, apparently not knowing her new boundaries, hesitated in defence and was severely attacked by the invading pair. This confusion may have been too much for her, for the next day she was found back in the sanctuary of her parents' territory where she remained a spinster during that year's breeding season. What happened to the widower? Within three days he was seen courting Big Red and ultimately they bred and raised three chicks. So here is another instance where a former family was reduced to a single pair.

This event raised another big question. Aunt Clara was now three years old and sexually mature, otherwise she wouldn't have attempted mating with the next door widower. Yet still she returned to her home territory, suppressed her urge to breed and aided her parents for another year. This is a most peculiar event in the animal kingdom where, according to current thought, animals breed as often and as fast as they can.

An observation from yet another territory showed us that kookaburras are sexually mature in one year. Birds in this particular territory were tagged in 1965 when two parents and one female auxiliary cooperated in raising three chicks. One of the chicks died when hit by a car, but the remaining two survived and resided within the parents' territory. Just before breeding the old auxiliary left the area, probably to find a mate of her own. The two juveniles, both males, functioned as helpers at the 1966 nest, incubating and feeding chicks as previously described. Then one of them was suddenly missing. A subsequent search found him in a territory about a quarter of a mile away where he was courting a tagged female whose mate had died. A month later, this year-old male became the father of three chicks.

Synthesising this information, we can now clarify our understanding of this unusual social system. Kookaburras reside in well-defined territories which may contain a single permanently-mated pair or a family group consisting of a mated pair and one or more auxiliary members. Auxiliaries are adult non-breeding birds which, instead of dispersing and breeding themselves, remain within their parents' territories year round and aid in territory defence, incubation of eggs, feeding and protecting of young. Some birds were known to have functioned as auxiliaries for three years, thus explaining the common occurrence of families with more than three members.

The next question to be raised is this. How can living in a family group suppress the normal breeding urge of these sexually mature auxiliaries? In human families this is done through socio-economic pressures but we cannot attribute such sophisticated *mores* to kookaburras. Although life within a

A mated pair with one auxiliary. ▼ ▲ *Fledgling with adult showing differences in the two age classes.*

kookaburra family is generally a peaceful one, we did note rather symbolic aggressive acts between various members. These aggressions were in the form of a sparring match in which two birds grasped bills and twisted and turned in a manner resembling Indian wrestling. These tests of strength lasted from thirty seconds to fifteen minutes and ended when the loser was either thrown off the perch or simply gave up and flew away. Young fledglings were seen to spend hours practising the technique alone. While quietly perched in heavy foliage they would peck at and twist various leaves and branches surrounding them. When about three months old and nearly independent, nest mates of the same sex would spar with each other.

By keeping track of all these actions, and noting who sparred with whom, who initiated the act and who lost, I was able to note a clear pattern of dominance hierarchy within the family. Interestingly enough, the sexes were separate in this hierarchy. Females sparred only with females and males with males. The adult breeding pair was always dominant. In any sparring match they were always the winners. The next most challenged bird in the group was the oldest auxiliary. In the male line this bird would challenge his father and loose but always won every match with his younger brothers. Between young nest mates, dominance was settled in their early sparring matches among themselves. They were always subordinate to older auxiliaries and to their father. The youngest fledglings took the brunt of bashes delivered by all older members of the same sex. These matches occurred most frequently when young fledglings were being taught to feed on their own. When an older member delivered food to the squawking youngster, the food was passed, then the older bird would spar and usually knock the younger off the perch. Whacks were also delivered when the greedy youngster would fly to a resting adult and persistently beg for food. In the early stages after fledging, the adult usually responded to food-begging by fetching a morsel. But as the months wore on, the youngster more often than not received a whack for its begging efforts and soon learned that it was easier to fetch food for itself. It is important to note that during this period the fledgling learnt its very subordinate position in the family. Only by waiting for a new batch of youngsters with which it would have a right to spar, could its position in the hierarchy be raised.

Auxiliaries can breed only if they possess their own territory (and a mate to share it, of course). This ownership entitles them to supreme dominance within their own plot of land. Until then, their subordinate position in the family hierarchy probably suppresses their urge to breed. Just how long a sexually mature kookaburra can remain subordinate is a matter of conjecture. After Aunt Clara's unsuccessful attempt at securing her own mate, she appeared resentful of her subordinate position. The sparring matches between her and her mother began to appear more testy and often verged on real violence. It

Young fledgling prodding its father for food.

would have been interesting to see what would have happened if the mother had not been the physically or psychologically stronger of the two.

With this new piece of information, we may add to our definition of the auxiliary system by saying that auxiliaries are non-breeding adult birds whose capacity to breed is suppressed by their subordinate position within the family hierarchy.

It might be best to conclude this chapter with a word or two about other birds which have a similar social system. Our knowledge of the existence of such a system in the bird world has only recently come to light with the advent of tagging techniques.

While helpers have been recorded at the nests of many species, few have been studied in enough detail to be able to state accurately just how many species employ auxiliaries as a constant feature of their biology. Perhaps the fairest assessment of this data can be made if we compare the families of birds both in Australia and around the world which have at least one genus employing auxiliaries. Of the one hundred and sixty-six families of birds in the world, twenty-five have genera with regular auxiliaries. Of these, nine are endemic to Australia. When it is borne in mind that of the 8,600 species of birds in the world, only six hundred and fifty occur in Australia, we certainly seem to be leading the world in this regard.

In addition to our nine endemics, three other families also have auxiliary genera but they occur outside Australia as well. For example, the family Rallidae is made up of water hens which are world wide in distribution and the young of some of these hens are known to pass food to members of later broods. But in the Tasmanian Native Hen, a flightless bird exclusive to Tasmania, Mr M. Ridpath found a well defined and highly coordinated auxiliary system which is very similar to that found in kookaburras.[15]

I will not attempt to give details of the life histories of all the Australian birds which display this remarkable type of sociality, but a few examples may be of interest.

Mr Ian Rowley discovered auxiliaries among Superb Blue Wrens, a species indigenous to this continent. In these birds only the young males stay the year round. They help the father feed the chicks and fledglings of the first brood while the female re-nests. The young from subsequent broods are then taken over and fed by the young of previous broods of the same season. The female's duty is largely reduced to laying and incubating eggs. Rowley reports that in one year he watched a female re-nest fourteen times.[16] That is a lot of baby wrens! In addition to the Superb Blue Wren, five other members of this same sub-family are known to have helpers.[5]

The Pied Butcher Bird also has auxiliaries. While Mr Thomas first noted this in 1951, Mr A. Watt of Lightning Ridge has done a study of tagged birds

Parent feeding young.

over a six year period and found that the juveniles from the previous year remain with their parents year round and help to feed the new batch of young. He does not know if they help to incubate but it is unlikely since they are immature birds, indicated by the distinct juvenile plumage they wear. When breeding is over and moult occurs, these juveniles acquire their adult plumage and are literally chased out of the parents' territory.

Mr Rowley found that the White-winged Chough is another Australian species to have helpers. In this species, several breeders and non-breeders may pile into one nest and communally rear the young.[17] We also know that this occurs in Apostle Birds, so named because of their communal ways, but they have not been studied in detail.[5,18] Australian Babblers are also social nesters and definitely have auxiliaries, but whether one or two breeding pairs contributes to the laying of the clutch is as yet uncertain.

The outstanding number of Australian birds showing this highly evolved social system leads us to wonder if there is something peculiar about the Australian environment to have given this form of sociality some special adaptive value.

Australia's winter climate is so mild that relatively few of our birds migrate to warmer quarters in the non-breeding season as is common for most Northern Hemisphere species. Dr Lack has pointed out that auxiliary systems could only evolve in species which are sedentary, because parents and young could not stay together if they had to migrate.[8] Sure enough, the one thing in common among these auxiliary species is their sedentary nature. Just how many more auxiliary species we will find simply depends on more bird watchers not only getting to know their subjects as individuals, but reporting their finds to the appropriate authority. With the help of modern tagging methods and with such organizations as the R.A.O.U. Nest Record Scheme and the C.S.I.R.O. Bird Banding Scheme, this is now a relatively easy and very rewarding task.

Kookaburra poised at the edge of the nesting hole with the next meal.

4. THE SIZE AND FUNCTION OF TERRITORY

The phenomenon of territory is a subject we are just now beginning to understand in depth. Territory is basically defined as any defended area necessary for survival of the species. The nature of this area may vary considerably from a substantial piece of ground defended all year round to a small invisible area around an individual which, if encroached upon, results in a hostile reaction. When we look at the broad spectrum of dispersal patterns employed by animals and man, we see that holding a permanent territory is only one of the many ways in which space is utilized for the benefit of the species' survival.

Some biologists have advanced the idea that the way a species utilizes space depends largely on the nature of its food supply.[3] Year round defence of a permanent piece of ground probably develops from the presence of permanent though predictably fluctuating food supplies. The species can best survive by building a fence around such a food resource and thereby exploit it more efficiently than if they searched randomly for it. Where food is more scattered throughout the year but concentrated in predictable amounts in the breeding season, animals may adopt a pattern called interspersion. Here, defence of an area for its food resources is advantageous only for the duration of the breeding season, so for the rest of the year the species roams in flocks exploiting food resources wherever they become available. Dr Brereton notes that this pattern is clearly seen in the Eastern Rosella.[3] At the extreme end of the spectrum are completely gregarious species which defend no area throughout the year except for a small area around themselves and the nest. This pattern of dispersion occurs when food is always widely scattered and often unpredictable. In order to survive, the species must be completely free from territorial bonds because they survive best by roaming wherever they find food.

While this is not meant to be a dissertation on dispersal patterns, the foregoing may help to give us some perspective into the basic function of territory. From this, we can perhaps understand why kookaburras defend a permanent territory. The range of prey species making up their diet certainly constitutes a permanent but predictably fluctuating food supply. By confining themselves to one defended

Thickly-wooded Belgrave study area. See the nest hole at the top of the centre tree.

area, kookaburras come to know their hunting grounds well and can procure a meal far more easily than if they foraged at random in less familiar areas. This would be especially true if food were in short supply. This site attachment function of territory is found in most predaceous species.

Kookaburra territories must not only contain a permanent food supply but they must also contain all the resources necessary for the birds' way of life. Some other requirements of their territories are that they must contain at least one hole in a tree or object large enough to nest in; a ground clearing frequented for food; some area of dense tree cover used as a roosting site and serve as a refuge site for fledglings. Oddly enough, in my study area, no erritory had a permanent supply of water. The birds seemed to get all they needed from their food. The lack of any of the above mentioned physical requirements will account for the absence of kookaburras.

Just how large an area does a kookaburra need to fulfil these requirements? We noted that family groups occupied far larger territories than did single pairs, so we measured territories before the breeding season and found that the size of the territory was significantly correlated with the number of birds in residence. In my study area, this size was around three acres per adult and juvenile bird. Thus, the smallest territories containing only a breeding pair were on the order of six acres and the largest, containing six birds, was eighteen acres. As we shall see later on, territory size changes just before breeding. Those groups that bred successfully the year before expanded their territories to accommodate the larger family. Expansion was always in the direction of those groups which lost members. We measured the amount of gain and loss and found that this too was on the order of three acres per bird. This discovery lead us to ask what factor or factors are responsible for determining this apparent requirement of three acres per bird.

Food availability must determine at least the minimum size of a territory. Intuitively we would expect to find kookaburras occupying larger territories in habitats of low food productivity and smaller territories in areas capable of high food productivity. Indeed, by comparison this seems to be true. The smallest territories I measured in a dry, open woodland of measurably lower productivity were about twice the size of the smallest territories found in the lush Belgrave study area.

Further evidence for the importance of food availability in determining the minimum size of a territory was seen directly within the study area since areas were expanded to accommodate the growing families. If a juvenile remained in its parents' territory and functioned as an auxiliary, that territory was enlarged probably to prevent the auxiliary from robbing its parents' food resources.

Three acres per bird is, however, larger than the minimum size required for

Map of the study area showing territorial boundaries, defence posts and nesting sites just prior to breeding in 1965.

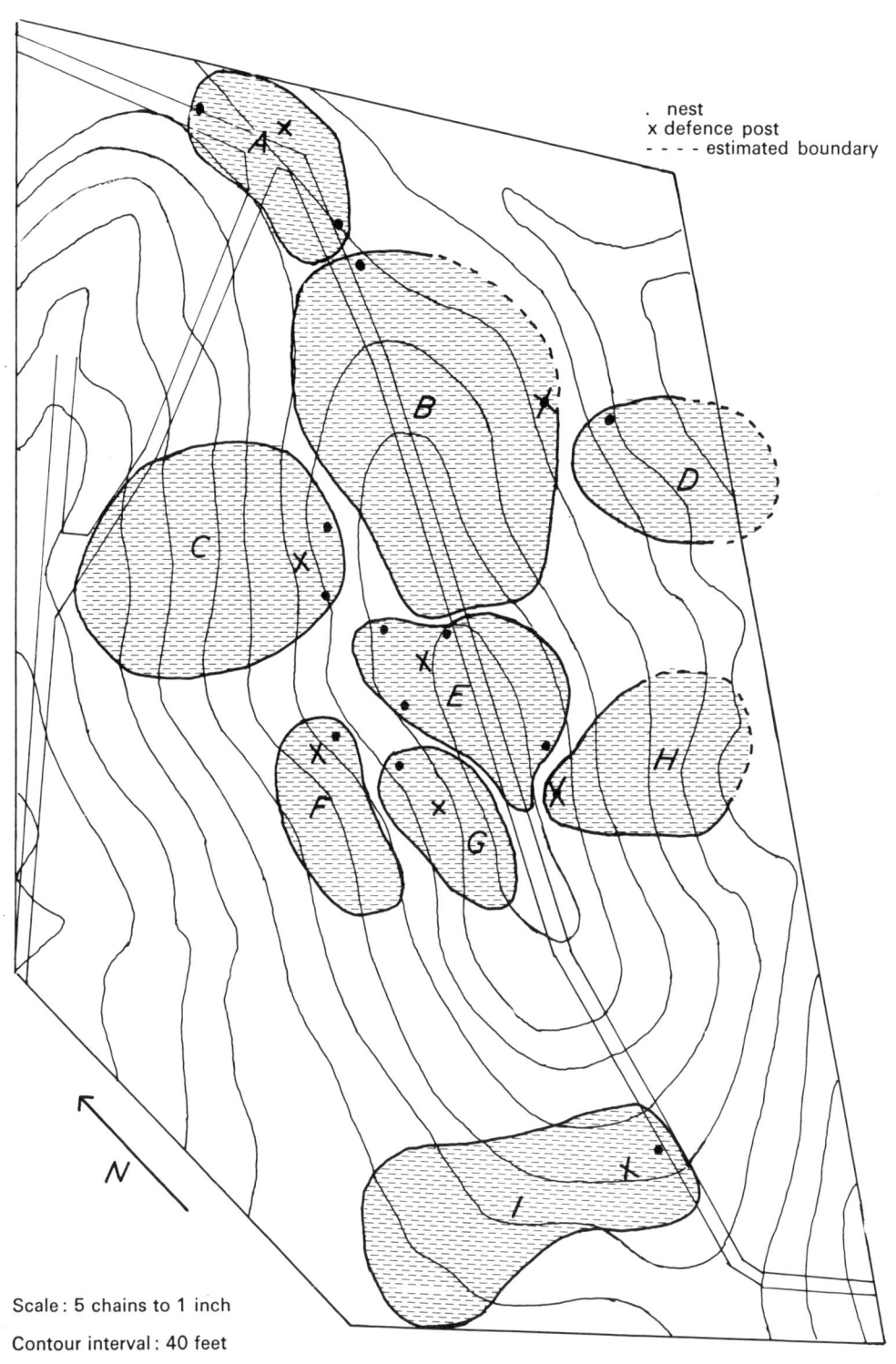

the survival of the birds present at the time the boundaries are adjusted. We can say this because territory size is determined before breeding, and although the predictable increase in spring food must cater for the chicks, this area must also support forthcoming juveniles when the breeding season is over. Thus, the area the birds defend in September, before breeding, must be capable of supporting a number of young not yet in existence.

Nor is this three acres per bird the maximum size a territory can be. In watching the pattern of adjustment over the two years, we noted that habitable gaps existed between some territories. Growing families certainly expanded and took over areas vacated by other families who lost members, but in some cases, this shift was not even. For example, two adjacent families lost members. A third family, which formerly shared a common boundary with both of them, expanded only in one direction leaving some twelve acres of good country vacant. Furthermore, no kookaburras entered that area that year. If food was the sole factor determining territory size, gaps such as these certainly would not be expected.

So far we know two facts; that territories are larger than required for the survival of the birds that defend them, and that territories are not as large as they could be if food determined their size. If food is not the sole determiner of size, what is? I suggest that size is determined primarily by the amount of space a kookaburra can successfully and efficiently defend.

Boundary adjustments are made during the peak of intense territorial defence just prior to the breeding season. And, as we shall soon see, this is also the time of dispersal when vagrant birds are searching for areas in which to establish territory (see Page 43). It is at this time when the group's ability to successfully defend their home ground is most severely challenged. Therefore, groups which are strong in numbers are better capable of defending larger boundaries than are small groups. Also, if a large group had a large territory one year and lost members the following year, it would probably not be successful in defending the same boundaries. In the face of pressure from expanding groups, the territory would contract to a size which could be successfully defended. We have seen this very thing happen in the study area.

When a family of four birds was reduced to a single breeding pair, the old boundary lines marking a twelve-acre territory were kept until September when another family challenged the pair for ownership. After one session of intense territorial display, the pair retreated and were next seen giving displays along borders marking a territory of 6.8 acres, an average two-bird holding. The area they left behind was not taken by the encroaching family even though it contained a good nest hole which the original pair had used the year before. It was left as a vacant gap which the pair may have given up simply because they could not defend it any longer.

Map showing boundaries, defence posts and nesting sites prior to breeding in 1966. There are more territories shown for this year because more families were observed and several territories were divided.

For example, territory B in 1965 was broken into B1 and B2 in 1966 as Big Red and her mate were unable to defend such a large area.

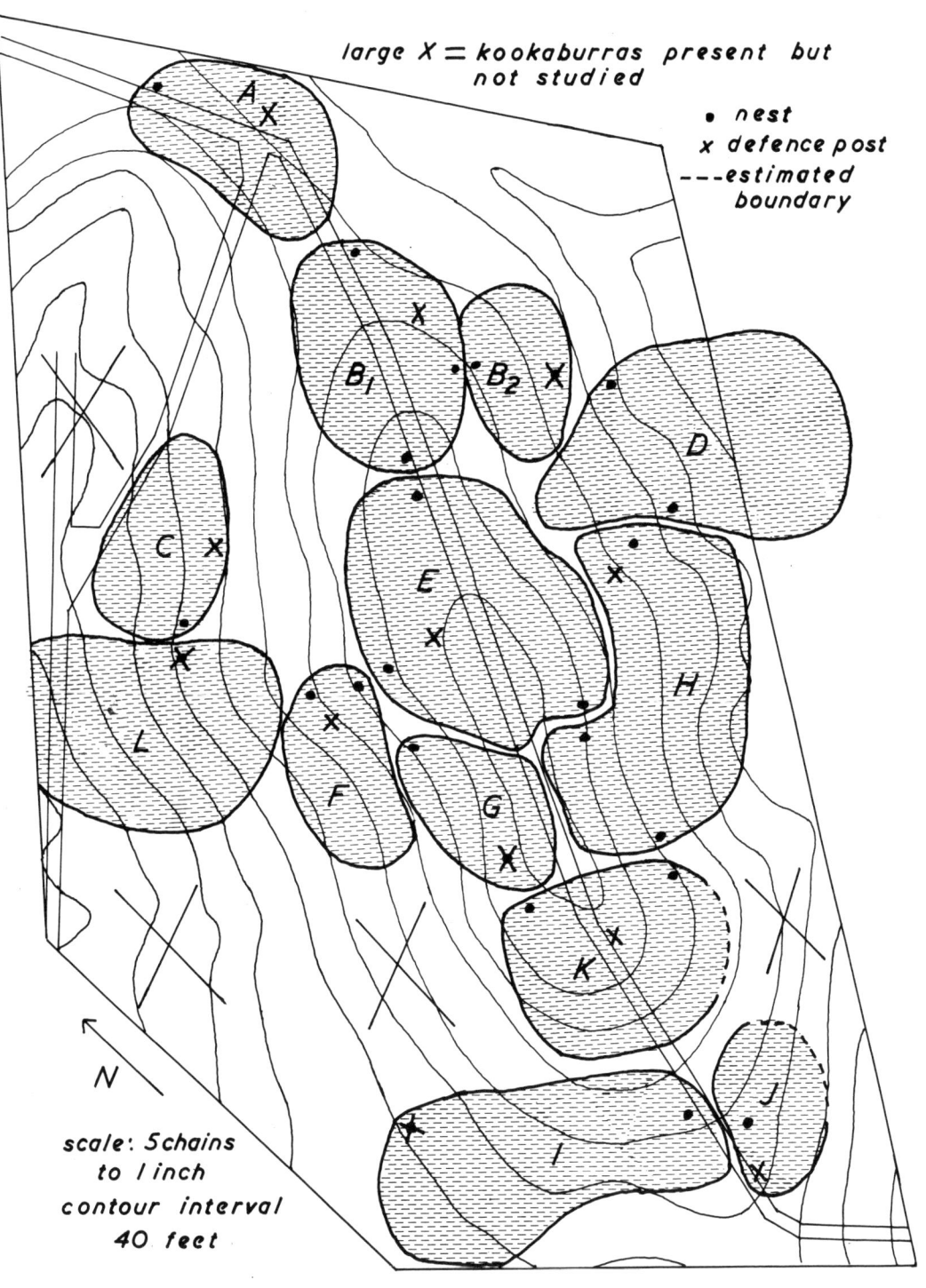

After we removed the breeding female from Big Red's territory, she and her father attempted to patrol their old boundaries. As you remember, they were not successful, for a new pair succeeded in taking over some six acres and even managed to win the group's former nest hole. But Big Red and her mate still had ample territory left. In fact, their original acreage was larger than average because it backed on to Sherbrooke Forest, a dense Mountain Ash forest generally unsuitable for kookaburras. Since this portion had no neighbours, Big Red's family could wander in to it but did not have to defend it. Thus, after the new pair claimed a six acre territory, Big Red and her mate still had some eighteen acres to patrol.

Aunt Clara's family were Big Red's southern neighbours. They had grown from the previous breeding season with two juvenile males remaining as auxiliaries, and so challenged Big Red and her mate for an additional six acres. With five birds against two, it didn't take long to decide the matter, so now Big Red's territory was reduced to twelve acres, still too much for an average two-bird holding but neither bird retreated to a defendable area as in the previous case. Sure enough, while attempting to patrol this large area, they were plagued by an invader. No amount of chasing, calling or fighting could remove this tenacious bird. He not only withstood days of the most intense aggressive attacks but began performing his own displays as if he owned the place. Big Red and her mate contracted their territory to 10.8 acres but to no avail, the invader was apparently there to stay. During September, while other pairs were courting and nesting, Big Red and her mate were still engaged in aggressive behaviour. Though they managed to rear three chicks to fledging, they appeared very tattered and stressed and often interrupted their parental duties to make another attack on the invader. Eventually, on 10 January, the invader disappeared from the area.

I don't know if the chicks' survival chances were hampered by this event but certainly the pair expended undue energy attempting to evict the invader; energy which could have been better spent on rearing healthy young. Perhaps if the pair had not attempted to defend a larger area than two birds could successfully and efficiently defend, this invasion would not have happened. These were the only birds in the study area that did attempt to hold a larger area than they could defend and they were the only group which failed to expel an invader.

From this evidence then, we have an hypothesis as to what factors determine the size of a kookaburra's territory. We cannot deny that food resources determine the minimum spatial requirement, but the optimum requirement, the three acres per bird, is probably determined behaviourally by the amount of space that can be defended.

You may wonder why the size of a territory is important. In almost all

The Size and Function of Territory   41

species, breeding rights belong to those who possess a territory. The number of pairs that can breed will be determined by the number and thus the size of territories that can be contained in any one area. This then places a ceiling on the number of birds in any propulation and also determines the reproductive potential, or number of young that can be produced. Any surplus birds that are produced are pushed to the periphery of the area where, occupying suboptimal territories, they either perish or are not very successful in reproducing.

For kookaburras, territory size is not such a simple matter. It is linked with the auxiliary system and thus affects the population dynamics of this species in another very positive way. You will remember that territory size was on the order of three acres per bird, whether that bird was a breeder or an auxiliary. Thus, auxiliaries, non-breeding adult birds, occupy the same optimum habitat and have the same territorial requirements as do breeding birds. By 'padding' this optimum space, auxiliaries are virtually reducing the reproductive potential of the population to a point below that expected if all territory occupants bred. So here territorial behaviour is acting through sociality as a method of birth control. This density-limiting function of territory is something relatively new and enlightening in the field of population regulation, and we shall have more to say about it later on.

Open woodland of the New England area.

5. VOCAL BEHAVIOUR

Kookaburras tend to be vocally rather than visually conspicuous. By living in medium-to-dense woodland and possessing a rather cryptic plumage (an advantage for such a predatory animal) it may be that kookaburras cannot see each other very well and so keep in contact more readily through vocal signals. They have one song, the familiar chorus of laughter, and six distinct calls. I consider the difference between a song and a call to be as follows.

Song is the most characteristic vocalization of the species. In most cases males advertise territorial ownership through their distinctive song which at the same time serves as a species-identifying character to the prospective female. From this we could say that in most species, song is essential for pair formation and reproduction. Call notes, on the other hand, are socially serviceable within the species concerned for they communicate particular information which serves to keep the group together and informed on each other's activities.

Much research went into determining the context, function, causation and origin of the song and calls, but rather than deal with this in detail, it will be more straightforward to summarize the findings by first defining the vocalization so that it can be recognized in the field, and then to discuss its function and any other relevant information. Since many of the kookaburra's vocal and visual signals fluctuate in frequency throughout the year, attention is drawn to the graph on page 43 which outlines the birds' annual pattern of activities.

The Laugh Song

Little need be said in the way of describing the famous laugh of the kookaburra. Many people round the world are familiar with it, thanks to the efforts of Hollywood film producers, who manage to convince us that kookaburras occur in any and all jungle settings, whether in South America, New Guinea or darkest Africa. To the uninitiated however, the song is best described as a full-throated, boisterous laugh. The cycle starts with a low chuckle of repetitive 'ooo' sounds lasting around two seconds. It rises in intensity to a loud laugh

Type of call	No. obs.	Time of year observed											
Laugh	741	J	F	M	A	M	Ju	J	A	S	O	N	D
Chuckle	285	██	██	██	██	██	██	██	██	██	██	██	██
Chuck	121						██	██	██	██	██	██	██
Squawk	99						██	██	██	██	██	██	██
Soft squawk	52							██	██	██	██	██	
Cackle	29	██	██	██	██	██	██	██	██	██	██	██	██
Kooaa	175	██	██	██	██	██	██	██	██	██	██	██	██
		J	F	M	A	M	Ju	J	A	S	O	N	D
ANNUAL ACTIVITY		Moult			Rise in defence					Breeding season			
							Dispersal period						

Graph showing patterns of annual activity and time of the year that the various calls were heard.

of repetitive 'ha ha ha' sounds from two to five seconds' duration then lowers again to a two-second chuckle like the first. This series of 'ooo' and 'ha ha ha' notes may be repeated many times. Finally it either stops abruptly, or fades away as the chuckle becomes less rapid.

The kookaburra's laughing song is usually a chorus with two or more birds sitting on the same perch joining it. I use 'chorus' loosely here, for certainly it is not synchronized in any harmonious manner. Once everyone has started with the introductory chuckle, each individual may launch into its own version of 'ooo' and 'ha ha ha' until the chorus gradually tails off. Sometimes I have even heard individuals improvise during a chorus. One breeding female in particular would be laughing along with her family then break out with a repeated 'who' at the end. She did this so often that I soon learned to tell she was present just by hearing her sing. Although laughing is predominantly a group activity, it may also be sung solo. Jacko, a kookaburra of the 1930's, made stage and radio fame by laughing alone at the request of its owner. In the field, if a kookaburra laughs alone, the rest of the group usually responds to it.

Choruses of song are heard year round but they occur more frequently a few months before the breeding season. Little song is heard during January and February when most kookaburras are moulting and therefore somewhat secretive.

Song is most pronounced in the twilight of morning and evening, giving the kookaburra the familiar name of Bushman's Clock. Anyone who has heard the almost ear-shattering din of kookaburras singing at these times of day will agree that it must be of some great importance to the bird's biology. The following observation will bring this point home to the unconvinced.

One evening just before the choruses broke out, cackle sounds indicating a fight were heard on the roosting perch. Four birds were present and the adult male and an auxiliary male were sparring with beaks locked and much wing boxing. During this battle the neighbouring territory gave its evening chorus. Meanwhile, the fighting birds, maintaining their hold on one another, became quiet and stopped fighting. When the group finished its round of song, all four birds gave their chorus, including the two opponents who, with beaks still grasped, threw back their heads and joined in. When the song finished, the fight continued just as energetically as before. The neighbouring group again rang out a song and the fight again stopped while all listened intently, but this time they did not respond. The battle resumed until the auxiliary was thrown off balance and flew to a lone perch with a reinforced lesson that he was still subordinate. Song obviously must be important if it can stop a fight.

By looking at a few more observations, the function of the laugh song will become clear to us. First, song at twilight involves all members of a family; it is never a solo. Sometimes during the breeding season an evening chorus

Vocal Behaviour

may not be heard, especially from territories where only a single pair reside. Since one bird broods the clutch at night, it may be that the lone member cannot sing at this time without its mate.

Though the owners of each territory give a most vociferous chorus, two groups seldom sing at the same time. Choruses are taken in turn and though a particular family may sing several times, it does so only before or after the birds of a neighbouring territory have sung. Since these choruses are sung on the roosting perch, one can locate the territories of the kookaburras in their area just by listening carefully at dawn and dusk.

Territorial boundaries are readjusted once a year during the three months before breeding, and it is at this time that song is most intense. One group, whose numbers had grown since the last period of adjustment, was attempting to enlarge its territory by encroaching on to some three acres of its neighbour's land. The neighbours had been less fortunate in breeding, and, with fewer members, were not very successful in the battle of land rights. One evening, members of the larger group, who had formerly roosted in the centre of their territory, moved *en masse* and roosted in the newly-claimed area where for over a week they advertised ownership by singing their morning and evening choruses. Thereafter, the loosers never again contested the area nor were they ever seen to enter it again.

Apart from these observations on morning and evening choruses, the context in which song was given throughout the day was also noted. Of the seven hundred and forty-one songs recorded, 66% were given near a territorial boundary and were responded to by a similar chorus of song from the birds of the neighbouring territory. Usually these sessions accompanied territorial defence displays. From this, it seems certain that the kookaburra's song functions to declare territory. Even though morning and evening choruses take place on the roosting site in the middle of the territory, their function seems to be the same.

As we noted in the observation on page 44, song is so important that it takes priority over a family squabble. This brings us to another of its probable functions. There is a definite relationship between singing duets and choruses and the social cohesion of the group. Males and females of many species sing in duet to maintain their pair bond.[24] In kookaburras, where all members of a family must peacefully coexist, social bonds between them may well be cemented with a rousing chorus of song.

There are situations not related to territorial behaviour when kookaburras laugh, indicating that there may be another function of song. The following explanation is only a subjective opinion, but these situations seemed to me to all have one thing in common. The birds appear tense or excited over something, usually some odd event which has just taken place. For example, if one kooka-

burra has captured a snake or some other big prize, others soon gather and hop around nervously on nearby perches. Then one may approach the holder of the prize and attempt to take it away from him in a vigorous tug-of-war fashion which can last several minutes until one or the other looses its hold on the object and gives up. Invariably, the remainder of the family breaks out in a raucous chorus of song.

I have seen four fledging events when the chick makes its big plunge from the nest. Every time, when the youngster alighted safely on the ground, the family gathered around it and broke out in peels of laugh song. Such a chorus would surely jeopardise the youngster's life since any predator in the area would probably be attracted by such a din and soon discover what all the fuss was about. Could fledging be such a tense and exciting event that the adults simply cannot help releasing some of this tension through song? Though I always hid behind a tree, perhaps the keen-eyed adults detected my presence at these delicate times and vented their increased nervousness through a chorus of song.

Situations like these two examples were so frequent that whenever I heard choruses away from the boundary lines, I got to know that something was happening and would drop everything to investigate. For this reason, I suggest that song may be an outlet for releasing a build-up of tension. We can see an element of this in territorial defence behaviours, for we know that defending territory is anything but a calm, relaxed affair. It may be that song given in these hectic situations may also be serving as a tension-releasing device, while at the same time functioning to declare ownership of a piece of land.

Now, before stepping over the border line and attributing human qualities to the kookaburra's laugh, let me clearly state that this is not the reason why kookaburras laugh when you trip over a log or fall victim to some other ludicrous accident. Nor, as some early pioneers thought, is theirs 'the call of wild spirits mocking misfortune'. Now that we know the biological function of the kookaburra's laugh song, we can chalk up all such fanciful notions to the realms of folklore.

The Calls

Kookaburras have six characteristic calls. Unlike the song, these are used only to communicate information among family members; neighbours do not respond to them. As we shall see, each has a particular function in relating information of a certain nature, and sometimes calls may be strung together in what could be considered crude sentences. Oddly enough, each call is related either to the laugh song or to the food-begging squawk. Short discreet calls relate very specific information such as 'look out'. They come from short concise parts of the song. Others relate broader categories of information

Dacelo gigas.

such as 'It's alright, you can't see me but I'm over here'. These come from less circumspect and more rambling parts of the song.

The first and most common call is the *chuckle*, and is the same sound as the introductory part of the song. Chuckles are given year round either as solos or choruses and can be given in flight. The main function of the chuckle is to locate another individual. When two kookaburras are not in visual contact you usually hear one give a chuckle, the other responds and then the initiator flies to the respondent. Since this call means either 'where are you?' or 'I am here', it establishes contact, and often other calls or behaviour patterns follow. Thus it is heard in many contexts, and may be a signal to relieve an incubating bird or an announcement to the chicks in the nest that someone has come with food.

When a strange kookaburra tries to invade an established territory it always does so with a low-pitched chuckle which sounds threatening. The owner responds in the same manner. From the behaviour that immediately follows, a low-pitched chuckle by an invader obviously means 'I am here, what are you going to do about it?' The owner replies 'I acknowledge your presence and you better leave or suffer the consequences'.

The second call, a *chuck*, is an abbreviated chuckle. It is repeated many times in a short staccato and may be given solo or by several birds simultaneously. This call is also a locating device but it is heard only during the breeding season, especially in connection with feeding the chicks and fledglings. Obviously there are advantages in having a specific locating call at this busy time of year, for with all members of a family taking an active role in nesting and feeding the young, group coordination must be at its prime.

Two other vocalizations heard only in the breeding season are the *squawk* and the *soft squawk*. These two calls are similar, one being derived from the other, so they are best discussed together. The squawk is a hoarse monosyllabic sound, low in pitch. It can be given singly or in a short series in which the first is slightly higher in pitch than the succeeding squawks. The soft squawk is similar but in a lower, softer tone and like the former, may be given solo.

The squawk is first heard intermittently in August just before the breeding season. Then it increases in frequency during the incubation period, and reaches its peak when chicks are present. Adults stop squawking when the chicks fledge, but then the youngsters adopt it as a most ear-grating form of food begging which persists for about three months after fledging.

The soft squawk on the other hand, is a courtship call strictly confined to the mated pair. One of the main forms of courtship in this species is nuptial feeding, where the male passes food to the female. The first sign that the breeding season is approaching is when kookaburras start to give the regular squawk call. The breeding female also begins with these harsh notes and she may even

Two male kookaburras with a female (centre) showing the differences in rump colour between the two sexes.

Kookaburra with Skink. (Frauca)   *Dacelo gigas.*

Three tagged chicks on the record sheet.

prod her mate as if begging for his courtship gift, but he refuses her completely until the tone of her squawk becomes soft. When it does, it most likely signals a physiological change in her which is perpetuated by courtship feeding. The similarity between this nuptial call and the food-begging call of the young is so striking that it is no wonder that the male responds by passing food.

But there is another significant function of this call which bears discussing. Because of the high degree of sociality in kookaburras, all members co-operate fully in all activities. The breeding female is just as aggressive in defending territory as the other members. Her help in this regard is valuable to the group, and so nothing must hamper her aggressiveness. At the same time, the male must get close enough to her to copulate. This soft squawk call and the passing of food symbolically reduces the female to a juvenile level. By giving it, she mentally becomes young and helpless and thus allows the male to approach and eventually mount. The rest of the time however, she is free to carry out her aggressive displays against her neighbours and other intruders who are frequent at this time of year. Notice too that this call is unique to the breeding pair, thus ensuring that only these two will be the parents in any family.

But why do other kookaburras in the family give the regular squawk before and during the breeding season? It is so different from the soft squawk that it cannot be confused with it, but I have an idea that it may have a somewhat similar function. The phenomenon of adult non-breeding birds being allowed to share nesting duties with the pair is so unusual that one would expect to find some special signal designed to reduce the natural aggressive tendencies of the pair and facilitate their tolerance. In addition to 'feed me', the food-begging squawk of the young also means 'I'm a wee defenceless baby, please don't hit me'. Certainly it is the most submissive call of the lot and no adult could respond aggressively to it. If non-breeding adults give this call, it is logical that the result would be the same. So, by giving it, non-breeding adults may be showing that they are not a threat to the pair and therefore the family can co-operate in a harmonious fashion.

The *cackle* is a repetitive call taken from the 'ha ha' part of the song, but with a short 'a'. Several birds may give it at once and it is heard in flight. When giving this call, the bird's plumage is sleeked so the large bill becomes prominent. This stance and call both indicate aggression. It is the kookaburra's war cry and is given just before an intruder or a potential predator is physically attacked. How I hated that ominous sound when I was caught red-handed tampering with a nest! Cackling kookaburras gathered and divebombed with furious gusto, sometimes hitting my back and neck. This is not a pleasant experience when one is clinging to a rope ladder thirty feet up a tree.

But I was not the only one to receive such treatment. Magpies and kookaburras frequently heckle one another. In my study area magpies always won,

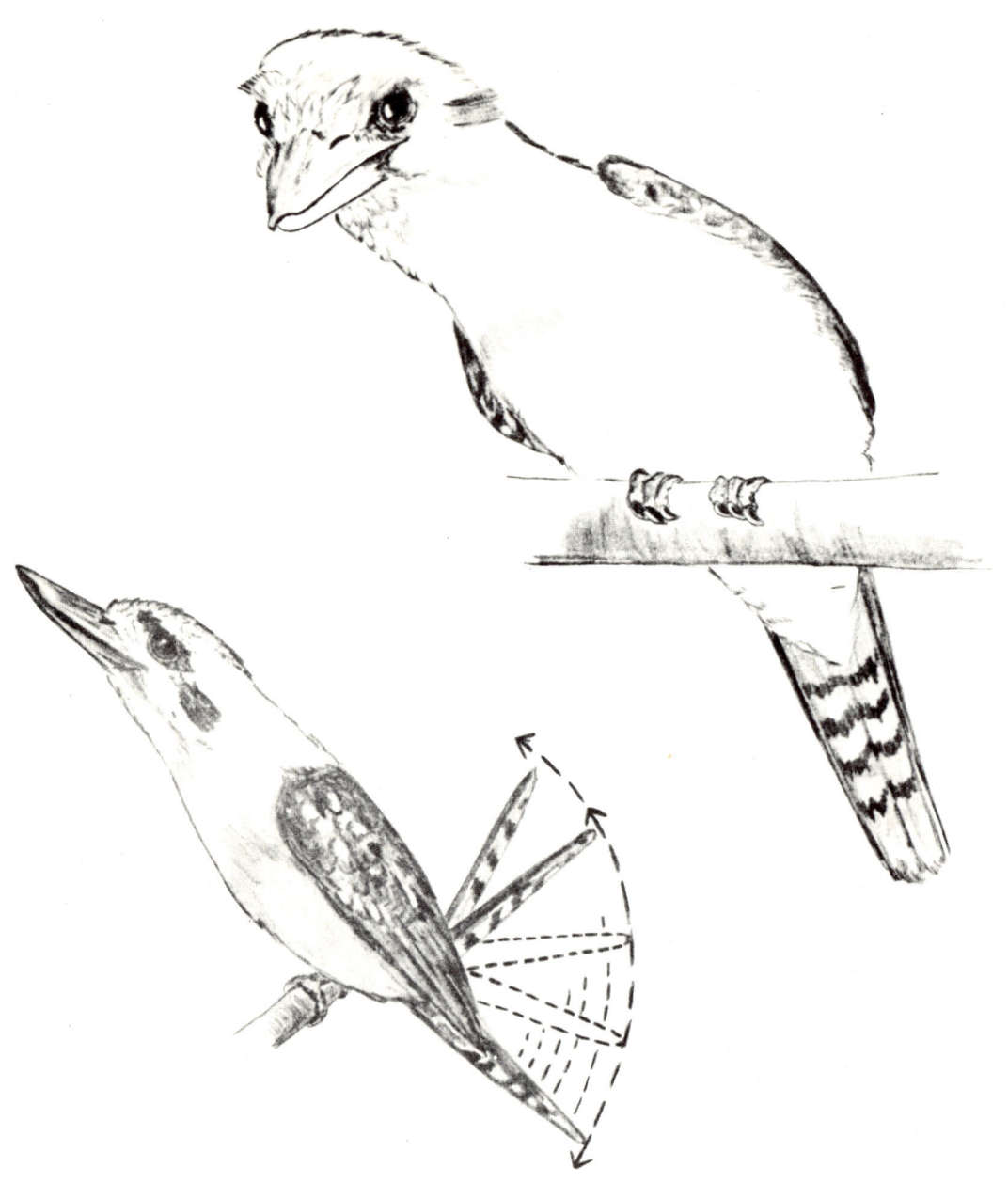

Line drawing illustrating bill pointing. (Hardie)
Line drawing illustrating tail pump given just before attacking. (Hardie)

and it was pathetically comical to see the ferocious look on a magpie as it closed in on the tail of a panic stricken kookaburra. The only time I've seen the tables turn was when magpies heckled a young fledgling. Cackles and sword-like bills appeared from everywhere. What a change to see that panic-stricken look on the magpies' faces as they turned tail and scattered.

The last call, the *kooaa*, is similar to that portion of the song which changes from the 'ooo' to the 'ha ha' of the laugh. Like the cackle, it is a short, concise sound from an equally concise part of the song and similarly has a warning function, meaning 'look out!' When given in a deep guttural fashion with the K very pronounced it means real danger—an eagle is overhead. Every kookaburra in the area stops what it is doing and assumes a special posture which conceals the bird perfectly from the overhead eye. (This posture is discussed more fully in the next chapter.)

The kooaa can also be soft, without the K. Here the bird is in normal position and often 'oooaas' in flight just before landing and before proceeding with some other call. It seems that this call also attracts the attention of the other kookaburras, but there is no cessation of activity or real alarm expressed. In both forms the kooaa is a warning or attention-getting device. In its harsh form it signals danger, in its soft form it draws the attention of the group and probably heralds a more specific call.

Let us summarise this chapter by listing the vocal repertoire of the kookaburra, along with the primary functions of each and the time of year they are heard.

Laugh song—advertises territorial ownership year round. The only vocalization between neighbours.

Chuckle—locates family members year round.

Chuck—locates family members during the breeding season.

Squawk—food begging, and a submissive call to reduce aggression among family members during the breeding season.

Soft squawk—courtship call of the mated pair, specifically to reduce the breeding female's aggression.

Cackle—signals aggression, a war cry heard year round before an attack.

Kooaa—a warning device heard year round which draws the attention of the group.

These signals are so straightforward that you should now be able to hear all of them in the field and in doing so, you will be able to understand most of what this animal is saying, which should allow you a more intimate insight into the kookaburra's way of life.

6. VISUAL BEHAVIOUR

The visual behaviour patterns of the kookaburra are relatively simple and so conspicuous that they are easy to observe. Whereas vocal behaviour is mainly oriented toward keeping the group together and synchronised, most visual behaviour communicates other information. We may consider these patterns in three broad classifications: general maintenance and food-getting behaviour, courtship behaviour, and the intriguing behaviour involved in territory defence.

General Behaviour

General behaviour is such a diffuse topic that we will consider only those patterns which are likely to be conspicuous and frequently observed.

Fear Kookaburras spend a great deal of time on the ground in search of food where, out of their arboreal element, they are vulnerable to predators and easily frightened. When caught unawares when it is too late to fly away, they become absolutely motionless, open their bills as wide as they can and raise their short crests straight up, giving the head a peculiar peaked shape. In this position the kookaburra looks larger and perhaps more menacing than it really is. We can only suppose that this posture functions to scare a predator away or at least to make it more hesitant about attacking.

Camouflage Wedge-tailed Eagles are known to prey on kookaburras. The only defence against such an avian enemy is to become as inconspicuous as possible which kookaburras do by assuming the 'stick pose'. Once an eagle is spotted, the guttural *kooaa* warns all woodland ears. As the message is passed along, kookaburras immediately stop all activity, point their bills skyward, and follow the passage of the bird of prey with their whole bodies, now stiffened like a rod and moving as a solid unit with the head. In this pose, and aided by the brown plumage on the back, a kookaburra should look exactly like a stick to the keen eye above. There is no variation in the stick pose and

As this kookaburra was offered a young snake, an aircraft passed overhead and apparently its shadow caused the young bird to assume a stick pose. (Frauca)

even young kookaburras can execute it perfectly upon their first encounter with an eagle, indicating that the behaviour is highly stereotyped. In this straightforward matter of life or death you can see that there is no room for plasticity in this behaviour.

We see some elements of the stick pose in another context. When an invader, with its familiar low-pitched *chuckle*, enters an occupied territory, the owner sallies with the same call but doesn't immediately challenge the rival. Instead, the owner remains inconspicuous on a branch, craning and stretching in every possible position as if to size up the opposition before taking immediate action. Sometimes the bird will lie in an almost horizontal position along the branch to get a good view. I have called these odd contortions 'bill pointing'. Once you see this behaviour, it is easy to suppose that this is related to the stick pose. All that is needed is the stiffening of the body and head into one unit and an orientation skyward. Thus bill pointing may be a ritualized form of the stick pose.

Roosting Kookaburras roost communally in two or three regularly-used roosting trees. As night approaches, the family gathers on the outer portion of a heavy branch some forty to fifty feet up where they render their evening chorus and follow with a session of preening and bill wiping. As they settle, kookaburras bunch up as close as they can till they look like one long line of feathers; only a count of tails reveals the numbers present. This bunching behaviour occurs year round so we cannot say that it is a thermo-regulatory device. But since the nocturnal Powerful Owl preys on kookaburras, bunching may be an anti-predator device. The vociferous evening chorus and preference for outermost branches for roosting would probably render individual kookaburras quite vulnerable if they were scattered. By bunching up as they do, they may appear too big to attack.

Feeding So far, stress has been laid on animals which prey on the kookaburra. Now let us look at the kookaburra as an animal which preys on others. Kingfishers have a particularly prominent bony ridge on the back of their skulls. Strong muscles are attached to this ridge which help to keep the neck rigid, a necessary adaptation in a diving bird. This remnant from aquatic days still persists but kookaburras now employ these strong muscles in killing prey, which they do by bashing their victims sharply against the perch. When the victim is dead, the bird throws its head back and in a jerk or two the food disappears down the gullet. Items with bones are run back and forth in the beak until supple enough to swallow, and bones and other indigestible bits are later brought up as a food pellet.

Kookaburras have phenomenally keen eyesight and will pounce on almost

Adult kookaburra in the stick pose.

Above: *A typical nest hole.*   Below: *A rather unusual and flamboyant nesting site.*

Kookaburra with Verreaux's Skink. (Frauca)

any living creature smaller than themselves, but in the main their prey consists of worms, snails, insects, freshwater crayfish, frogs, lizards, snakes and occasionally small birds and rodents. To get a fuller picture of the kookaburra's diet, I gathered the following data from observations made on items eaten mainly during the breeding season. Lizards and snakes constituted 35% of their diet; insects—32%; earthworms—15%; crayfish—8%; human handouts—7% and rodents—1%. A total of 55% of the diet is composed of invertebrates, mainly insects, so that kookaburras are properly called insectivorous as well as carnivorous. As to the latter, you can see that lizards and snakes are highest on the list.

Now for an outside opinion. I reviewed sixty-six articles in scientific publications dealing with the kookaburra's diet. Forty reported the eating of rodents, lizards, snakes, insects and worms and only eighteen reported the eating of small birds. Two of these articles told how kookaburras aided substantially in reducing insect outbreaks.

Those who regard the kookaburra as a villain may readily point to the eighteen articles referring to the eating of small birds. It cannot be denied that kookaburras occasionally prey on others of the avian world. Though I never saw this during my study, I would imagine that where drought conditions reduce its preferred prey of insects and reptiles, the kookaburra may have to turn to small birds to survive. Kookaburras however, are not very adept at manoeuvring on the wing and are downright clumsy when it comes to moving around in dense scrub. Since most small birds are sheltered in this type of vegetation, kookaburras would have little success in catching them. Only the slow and the sick would be vulnerable and would naturally fall prey to any carnivore; in most cases any carnivore is quicker than a kookaburra.

Tales of kookaburras and snakes rank high in folklore. There is still some mystery about the seemingly avid way in which kookaburras attack snakes but let us again turn to facts on the subject. Kookaburras are great predators of snakes, especially young ones. Snakes hatched in the spring time make marvellous meals for kookaburra chicks. One afternoon I was watching a family busy with its endless duty of fetching and shoving food down hungry little gullets. The monotony of the shuttle service was suddenly relieved by an excited *chuckle* which brought the family's attention to one spot in the forest. After a round of laughter, each of the five members appeared at the nest with a small three-inch snake. The excitement persisted for the next hour as snake after snake hit the pits of hungry stomachs. Observations similar to this were common during the two breeding seasons I studied, giving us convincing evidence that kookaburras play a large role in reducing the snake population.

How big a snake can a kookaburra kill? Unfortunately, all the fascinating

Kookaburra alighting at edge of nest hole with a large insect. (Slater)

stories stop when the kookaburra has killed the snake and none carry on to say what the bird eventually did with it. But I have made several observations and carried out two experiments which may be of interest. Once I found the posterior eight inches of snake hanging out of a twenty-eight-day old chick's beak. The snake was estimated to have been eighteen inches long. So, during the breeding season we know that large snakes may be fed to youngsters who, in the protection of the nest, can be pacified for several days with one long, slowly-digested meal.

Evidence suggests that when no youngsters are around, kookaburras kill but do not eat large snakes or rodents. Presented with a dead three-foot Brown Snake, a wild kookaburra was keenly interested and stared at it for forty-five minutes but did not pounce. The minute we attached a bit of string to it and made it slither along the track the bird was on it in a flash, grabbed it behind the head and thrashed it violently. The bird then paused for a second and, apparently realising the snake was limp, dropped it and flew away.

I put a live laboratory rat on the floor of an aviary once and could barely stand back quickly enough before a captive kookaburra pounced, grabbed the neck, and violently thrashed the animal exactly as with a snake. Again, once the rat was limp, the bird dropped it and paid no further attention to it. This behaviour led us to believe that kookaburras sometimes kill larger items of prey than they can eat. Since I do not know if the birds regard these large animals as a threat to their own survival I cannot suggest why they do it. The birds haven't the equipment to dismember these items so they are left as a nice piece of carrion for some other animal. I have never seen a kookaburra fly high into the air and drop a snake to the ground to facilitate a kill but reliable observers say this is so.

To conclude this section on feeding behaviour I will put in a claim for the beneficial job kookaburras do for humans through their relish for insects and reptiles. The odd instance of occasionally eating small birds and robbing goldfish ponds must be forgiven them. After all, the kookaburra is a link in the food web; it preys upon smaller animals and in turn is preyed upon by larger ones. Nature is thus balanced and should be left so.

Courtship Behaviour

We have already touched on this fascinating behaviour when we discussed the *soft squawk* call. But there is much more to it than that. Since kookaburras are permanently mated there is no need for elaborate nuptial displays. But, if reproduction is to occur, the pair must have some forms of behaviour, apart from those common to the family, in order to reinforce their pair bond and to stimulate a physiological readiness to breed. This is done in two ways, through

This photograph illustrates the kookaburra's impressive wing span. (Slater)

courtship feeding and the nest-showing ceremony.

We have already said much about courtship feeding and touched on its significance. Let me just add that it occurs as much as forty-four days before and six days after the laying of the first egg, the male passing more and more food to his mate as egg-laying time approaches. The quantity of food he passes is so substantial that as egg-laying approaches, he often gathers more food for her than himself.

David Lack, a famous ornithologist, has looked at the relationship between food-gathering and the time of egg-laying. He has shown that females lay eggs at such a time to ensure that food will be at its peak of abundance when the clutch hatches. This means that at the time of laying, food may not be as plentiful as it will be when the young hatch. But still the female must find enough nourishment to be able to form eggs and it is here that courtship feeding is functionally useful. The male's nuptial gifts actually supplement the female's diet so much that, without his help, she may be hard pressed to find enough egg-forming food on her own. This shows us that courtship feeding plays a bigger role in reproduction than the symbolic ceremony we once thought it was.[7]

The nest-showing ceremony is the second component of courtship and it occurs as much as forty days before egg laying. As in courtship feeding, it is accompanied by the *soft squawk* call.

Kookaburras re-nest in the same hole year after year if it is still vacant. Possums or bees often move into these roomy cavities, in which case the birds must scout around for another. But nest-showing ceremonies occur whether it is an old or new nest. If it is an old hole, the pair spend their time cleaning it out or just sitting in it. For example, a pair made a seventeen-minute visit to their old nest hole thirty days before the first egg was laid. Both arrived on a commonly used perch in front of the hole and gave a *soft squawk*. The female went in, and for six minutes she was seen poking the floor of the cavity, presumably rearranging the chips and dust naturally found there. The male waited outside on the perch and when he gave a *soft squawk*, she came out and joined him. He then went in the hole and sat quietly for thirty seconds. When he came out, the two sat on the perch and gave intermittent *soft squawks* for seven minutes after which the female returned to the hole and spent another three minutes prodding and rearranging. On her return the male went in and sat quietly for one minute. Then both left the area of the nest. This sort of nest visit goes on about once a day until laying starts.

Even if the old hole is vacant the pair will sometimes perform nest-showing ceremonies at several other holes. As you can imagine, this is a trying time for the observer. I always kept my fingers crossed hoping that the pair would decide that their old hole thirty feet up would do in preference to a new one fifty feet

Courtship feeding.

up. In these cases my luck always held. But the game was really on if a pair had to choose and remodel a new hole, for the birds spent an equal amount of time in any of several nests. As egg-laying approached however, their time and energies become centred on the preferred hole.

Much remodelling can be done if the entrance to the nest is not directly in front of the cavity. In a preliminary study of kookaburras, Mr Hindwood noted that the cavity was always in line with the entrance and he showed how this was necessary for nest sanitation.[6] Since young kookaburras excrete their waste out the nest hole, the cavity would soon become fouled if there was a bend tunnel between it and the hole to the outside. Observations during a set of nest-showing ceremonies showed Mr Hindwood's statement to be true. One pair had to find a new nest and chose one with a hole behind which an eight-inch tunnel bent sharply to the right before opening into a twelve-inch cavity. During six nest-showing ceremonies the pair chiselled the tunnel away so that the entire twenty inches formed one large chamber which opened directly to the outside.

This pair also showed me how necessary it was for both birds to take part in the nest-showing ceremony. The male did most of the chiselling and when the pair arrived on the perch the female's *soft squawk* seemed to entice him to go in where he worked for sessions often lasting twenty minutes or so. He would frequently poke his head out, but the female waiting on the perch would *soft squawk* and he would return immediately to his duty. If he looked out and found that she had left the perch, he would also leave and return only if she did.

Nest-showing ceremonies finished about four days before egg-laying but sometimes during this interim one of the pair would sneak back alone for a quiet sit which often lasted several minutes. This was not considered a part of the ceremony, since the individual was alone. These quiet visits simply indicated the bird's physiological readiness to incubate.

Nest-showing ceremonies are found in many species and it is agreed that they most likely condition the pair to the nest site. In other words, of all the holes in a territory the pair learns which one is to be the nest.

The final stage of courtship is copulation. There was no special ceremony involved in this behaviour but eight of the eleven copulations I saw occurred on the perch opposite the nest hole or very near it.

Territorial Defence Behaviour

As we discussed earlier, possession of a territory in which the bird is dominant appears to be a requisite for breeding. Auxiliaries are kept from breeding through their subordinate position and they are subordinate because they do

Kookaburra with a snake. (Garston)

With its crest up, this kookaburra demonstrates the fright posture. (Frauca)

not own their own territory. However, the drive to defend territory is so strong that auxiliaries and even fledglings aid the dominant pair in patrolling the boundaries and advertising ownership. Thus defence is truly a family activity, and apart from any other functions, it probably plays a strong role in enhancing social bonds which keep family members together. After all, we all know that there is nothing better than an outside threat on one's homesite to calm the squabbles from within and strengthen family cohesion.

I defined a territory simply as a defended area and defence begins at the boundary line between two neighbouring territories. Except for the period when dispersal or territorial enlargement takes place, no bird crosses the invisible line into another's property. Even when defence is at its lowest point during moult, the juiciest of morsels thrown over the border could not entice a bird to cross the invisible line, even though the neighbours were out of sight.

Kookaburras spend a lot of time defending their boundaries all year round. The displays involved are the most complex of their behavioural repertoire and thus they are the most fascinating to watch. The whole group co-operates in performing three displays which have a common origin but differ in the amount of hostility expressed, this being determined by the type of interloper toward whom the display is directed. We can classify interlopers as opponents, marauders and invaders. Neighbouring groups so often display to each other that there is little doubt that they recognize one another individually, and providing that neighbours remain within their respective boundaries, the display is not very hostile. Familiar neighbours then are classified as opponents.

There is a different, more hostile display given before a strange vagrant who passes through a territory and, upon seeing that it is filled, moves on as quickly as possible. These birds are called marauders. An invader, on the other hand, actually enters the territory in defiance of the owners' very hostile display and means to stay and challenge ownership. Except in two cases, marauders and invaders were always single birds of either sex, and they were seen only during the period of dispersal from June to September.

Defence displays may be performed within the territory but they are more common at the boundary. In either place, however, the display is performed on regularly-used defence posts, which are simply trees containing a scar or hole in the trunk. Between each defence post and the boundary is a perch where members of the group gather. There are two posts, one on either side of the territorial border which serves to mark the boundary between two opposing groups. These posts are ten to fifty yards apart and usually opposite or at least within clear view of each other. The stimulus to gather at the defence post appears to be the sight or sound of opponents near the boundary. Defence within the territory seems to be triggered more often by the laugh song of an opponent whereas defence at the border is triggered more by the sight of the opponent.

It is interesting to note the protocol associated with defence displays. For example, groups most commonly display to groups and conversely, an individual may display to another lone individual. With one exception, I have never seen a lone bird display to a group or vice versa. A group may amass for conflict, but upon seeing that the opponent is alone, only one bird challenges while the others sit back and perhaps lend moral support only by a chorus of song. Even the most hostile invader is met by only one member of a family. While this appears to even out the match, it certainly does not seem to be the most expedient means of evicting a challenger.

Let us now discuss the three types of territorial defence displays. The first and most common type is the *trapeze display*. It is so named because the birds fly to and fro from perch to scar, passing each other in mid air just like trapeze artists in a circus. The display starts as the birds of two opposing groups gather on their respective defence posts amid bursts of laughter and chuckles. Then a few members start to trapeze fly. One bird flies to the scar or hole and may momentarily poke its head into it, giving a chuckle. As the first bird returns to its perch, a second bird is on its way to the hole. The remainder of the group sit on the perch and give a chorus of song. When the two fliers have returned, the opponents, who have been watching their neighbours, then perform in a similar manner. During the excitement of an intense trapeze display, the two groups can get out of phase, so that both groups are trapeze flying and laughing at the same time; however, some synchrony is the usual rule. The fury of this display decreases over several minutes until hostility has been vented and both groups fly off.

When we analyse this behaviour in the light of the basic drives of the bird we see here a simple component of ritualised attack and escape. It is probably basic to all territorial animals that when on their own ground their tendency to attack is far greater than their tendency to escape. However, as the animal moves closer and closer to its boundary, its tendency to escape becomes stronger but the attack component is not swamped. When completely out of familiar surroundings, its escape tendencies are strongest and completely overcome any tendency to attack. Thus, the animal flees back to its territory. Once on home ground, the attack tendencies again take over. We are all familiar with these sensations for we certainly feel braver on home territory than we do in strange places.

We can see this pattern clearly in the trapeze display. The flying to and fro may be ritualised attack and escape. The flight toward the boundary in the direction of the opponents symbolises attack, and once near the tenuous dividing line escape takes over and the bird flies back to safer ground away from the boundary. Little hostility is expressed because the birds do not actually cross the boundary. To put it more simply, they are not provoked enough to make

Kookaburra demonstrating a fright posture. (Frauca)

more than a threatening gesture of invading another's territory.

The second display expresses more hostility, and aptly it is seen only during June and September, the time of year when boundaries are most carefully guarded from both marauding birds and familiar opponents who are attempting to expand their territories where possible. With increased hostility, defence often takes the form of a chase. If a marauder passes into a territory, he usually approaches flying very high over the tree tops. Upon seeing this vagrant, the owners burst out in song; then one member launches into a high, fast flight of pursuit which ends when the marauder is safely on the other side of the boundary.

Components of this basic chase are seen in a very ritualized behaviour called a *circle flight*. This display usually occurs between two opposing groups who are contesting with one another for an extra bit of land. Circle flights usually break out during an intense trapeze display where, instead of flying backwards and forwards from the boundary as in a trapeze flight, the birds express their increased tendency to attack by actually crossing the boundary. The flight from scar to perch doesn't stop and the bird flies high and fast over the tree tops some 200 yards into the neighbour's territory. This classifies the interloper as a marauder to the owners, and one of them launches off in a chase. Being pursued when so far from home base, the pseudo-marauder soon develops a strong impulse to escape and circles back to its own defence post. The pursuer however, now has a strong attack tendency which was not vented when the opponent left, so it continues past its boundary in a flight over the opponent's territory. The owners, who were once aggressors, are now defenders so they pursue the pseudo-marauder back to the boundary. Thus, circle flights trace large figure of eights high above the trees as each group vents its aggressive tendencies by invading one another's territories in turn. Of course, during these flights, choruses of laughter are given with great fervour by the remaining members of the group. As in trapeze flights, the display gradually peters out and the birds eventually go their own way.

As the breeding season gets closer, homeless birds who have not been able to find a vacant territory become more tenacious and often try to force their way into occupied territory. This type of invasion sometimes results in the third form of territorial defence, a physical attack. Since strangers of any sort are not permitted, these invaders play a fool's game. After reciprocal *low chuckles*, the owner sizes up the situation by bill-pointing, then assumes a sleek posture so that the bill appears as a formidable weapon. Then, with a *cackle*, the very hostile owner swoops and attacks the invader. With bills grasped the two wheel and tumble to the ground where the invader is beaten, often till blood is drawn. In most cases the invader invariably loses and flies off at the first opportunity.

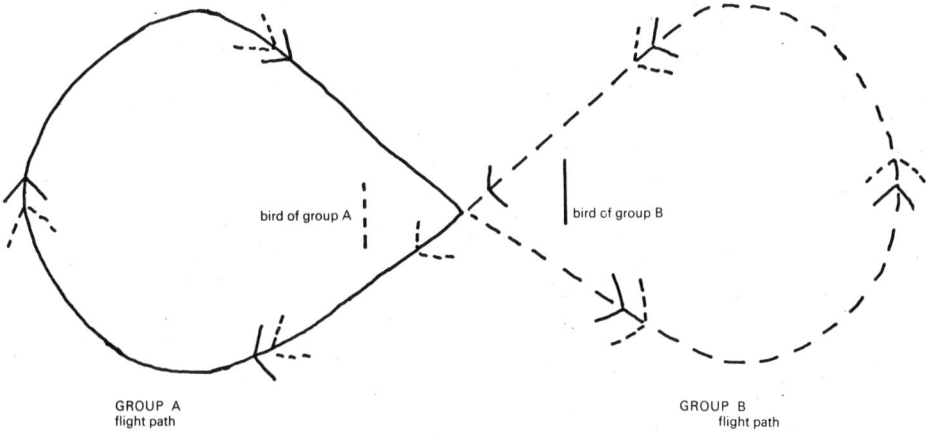

Diagram showing a circle flight.

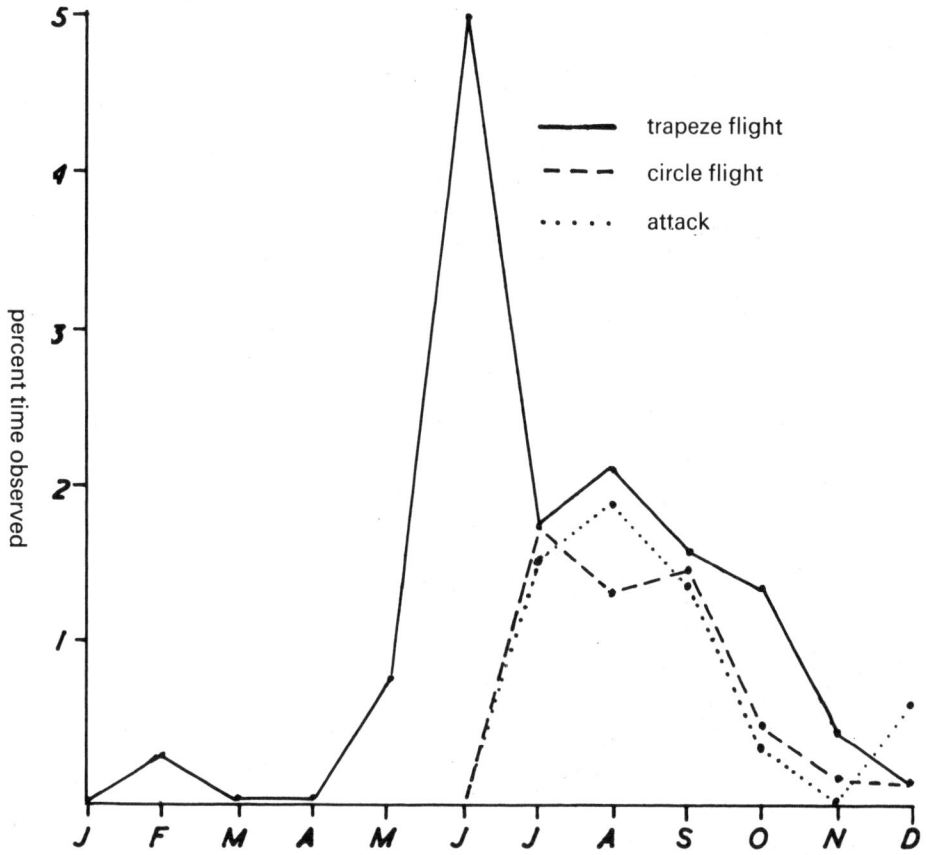

Graph showing frequency of the various territorial displays.

One October afternoon an invader announced its location with a *low chuckle*. It was sitting near the boundary of two neighbouring territories but just inside one of them. The male owner advanced, alighted near the invader and gave the tail pump posture for some thirty seconds. He then flew to his mate and both gave a *low chuckle*. The male again advanced near the intruder and 'bill-pointed'. Two minutes passed, then the male sleeked his plumage, flew to the intruder and attacked it by grabbing its beak. Both birds spun to the ground where the male started attacking the back of the intruder's neck. The intruder attempted to fly away but the male hung on and in the scuffle the two tumbled over the boundary line. The neighbouring male, who had been watching all of this, glided down and also attacked the invader. Both males then chased the outsider down the boundary line. Each split in opposite directions at the end of the boundary and flew to their respective territories while the invader continued straight on into unoccupied property. Although the second male was defending his territory when the two fighting birds crossed over the boundary, it is interesting that he attacked the intruder, not his normal opponent.

Just how severe these battles are is a matter of conjecture. The Victorian Fisheries and Wildlife Department receive many injured kookaburras at this time of year. Those with broken limbs are probably vagrant birds who met with natural accidents, but those with blood stains about the head and breast are suspected invaders who have lost battles. The department has received two birds which had their entire lower bills torn off at the base. These were most certainly invaders who learned a lesson the very hard way. Fortunately, this third form of territorial defence, physical attack, does not happen too often.

Knowing this ultimate expression of hostility we can easily say that if it were the only form of territorial defence, the birds would be so ragged and weary that they would not have much success at reproduction. Thus, other displays have evolved which symbolically take the place of actual attack and escape. A familiar opponent does not pose a serious threat during most of the year, so a mild trapeze display serves as a fist shaken to reinforce the boundary. The half-hearted attempts at invasion by a marauder are taken care of by a chase and marauding neighbours are dealt with by a circle flight or ritualized chase. Thus, a physical fight is necessary only in cases of outright invasion.

Let us look briefly at the origin of the displays themselves. We have already been discussing this in the nature of the ritualised attack and escape, symbolised by the flight toward an opponent and then away. But why does the kookaburra jab at the scar or hole in a trapeze flight? First we must ask what the bird is defending. It is not the mate since both co-operate in defence, nor is it an area in the strictest sense, since display is given within the area as well as on its periphery. After studying several hole-nesting species, von Haartman suggested that because holes were a limiting factor in the environment, competition for

Kookaburra approaching nest hole with food.

them is keen and hole-nesting birds tend to fight for possession of a hole rather than a territorial area.[23] Among kookaburras, nest holes are usually placed near a boundary indicating that a hole may be the primary object which they fight for and defend. Certainly the most likely place where ownership of a hole would be challenged by another kookaburra would be on the periphery of an area where two opposing groups meet. This is where most trapeze flights take place and the boundary is demarked. Thus, by defending real or symbolic nest holes, kookaburras acquire an area in which to live.

Before ending this discussion on territorial displays, two common questions need answering. First, why do kookaburras raise their tails upon alighting on a perch? We notice that before resorting to some hostile action, such as a chase or a fight, the owner of a territory sleeks its plumage and starts to pump its tail up and down. The pump is slow and deliberate as the closed tail is lifted about four to six times. With each upward movement the angle decreases so that by the sixth time the tail barely moves. This pattern may be repeated until the particular defence display occurs. In this context, tail pumping looks like an expression of hostility. Some of the energy about to be expended in the forthcoming action may be released a little by the tail pump.

Throughout the year we often see kookaburras lift their tails after alighting, particularly after long flights. Here the tail is lifted just once but may remain upright for a second or two. It is not a balancing movement since it does not always occur and it is often delayed a second or two after landing. We also notice that in an unusually raucous chorus of laughter the birds' tails go up as the climax of the song is reached. From these and the above observations I get the feeling that the 'tail up' pose and tail pumping are related. Like a cat swishing its tail before pouncing on its prey, tail movements in kookaburras may serve to release a build up of tension. Whether these movements also serve as a signal to others of the species I do not know.

The second question is why kookaburras crash into pane glass windows. This inquiry always comes between July and September. After reading this chapter you can probably answer this query as easily as I can. The bird sees its own image and regards it as an invader which must be attacked.

Many times the image is attacked with such force that windows are broken and the kookaburras badly injure themselves. Until recently, neither Fisheries and Wildlife nor myself could offer much in the way of a solution to house-holders plagued by these single-minded birds. But Mrs Cunningham of Palm Beach, N.S.W. has found an answer for us. She hung bright oddments from the eaves of her house so they dangled in front of the window and noted that the kookaburra seemed distracted by these objects and diverted its attack at the last minute. Mrs Cunningham wrote to say that her decorated windows so successfully discouraged her troublesome kookaburra that he began bashing the neighbours' windows instead. As each neighbour copied Mrs Cunningham's idea, the thwarted but persistent bird moved on to other houses. To add a bit of flair, householders began to be creative about their oddments which included highly decorative scarecrows, aluminium pie tins suspended by tinsel and even Christmas baubles. As you can imagine, it wasn't long before the neighbourhood began to take on a very bizarre appearance. Although this sight may have left many a passer-by puzzled, at least no one had to replace expensive pane glass windows that year.

7. BREEDING BIOLOGY

The course of any species' evolution depends solely on the leaving of viable offspring. Those individuals which have found a way to do this even a little bit better than others will be the best survivors and the pattern they adopt for leaving better offspring will lessen the chances of the species becoming extinct.

Although this concept of evolution is very easy to understand, we sometimes carry its simplicity too far by confusing or forgetting a few vital words of its basic definition. For instance, the idea of survival of the fittest often connotates individuals competing with other individuals in a 'red in tooth and claw' fashion. This is not true, for it is the survival of the species that matters most, not necessarily the individual. Sometimes individuals must put their own survival in jeopardy for the sake of enhancing the chances of other members of the group or population. The feigned injury behaviour of a female Wood Duck to lure a predator towards her and away from her chicks is a good example of this. Auxiliaries who feed and protect young that are not their own may be another example. It is the survival of the fittest group, not the individual that allows altruism to have adaptive value.

Another commonly misconstrued idea is that survival of the fittest plays its largest role in the reproductive phase of a species' life cycle. We often think that as long as the animal leaves as many offspring as it can, the survival of the species is ensured. This is not necessarily true. Extinction is thwarted only if the offspring are fit enough to eventually reproduce themselves and in turn leave viable progeny. An animal that cannot survive to procreate, plays no role in keeping its species on the face of the earth.

We must also remember that the survival of those doing the breeding is just as important as the survival of the young they bear because a good breeder will leave more and healthier offspring than a poor one. Thus, in kookaburras we may expect to find that pairs with auxiliaries to help in nesting duties will be less stressed and therefore will do a better job in rearing young than pairs without help, and from this we may expect that parents in families have better chances of survival during this hectic period than solitary pairs.

The author demonstrates her climbing ability and also the perspective on the height (30ft) and position of an average nest. This is the same nesting site shown at the top of the photograph on page 35.

Before this study, the basics of the kookaburra's breeding biology had been gleaned mainly from pairs nesting in captivity. These studies could not have approached this species' breeding biology from the approach we are going to take. This approach is to test the principles of evolution; the survival of the fittest group through the leaving of viable offspring. Because kookaburras are found both in solitary pairs and in family groups, we have a golden opportunity for such a test by way of comparison. If families exercise these principles better than pairs, we can see why sociality has become such an integral part of their way of life. So, throughout this chapter our basic aim is to seek the answer to one question. What is the adaptive value of the kookaburras' auxiliary system? As we shall see, the answer will be found in many unexpected corners.

Nests, Eggs, and Incubation

We have compiled data from the C.S.I.R.O. Bird Banding Scheme, the R.A.O.U. Nest Record Scheme and our own figures and found that kookaburras lay eggs between September and December. Oddly enough, the starting date does not seem to vary over 12° of latitude. We must be careful with this statement however, since it may be that bird watchers don't become active until September. At any rate, over two consecutive seasons in the study area, kookaburras started at that time. Families always started first and laid eggs over a longer period than did pairs.

Kookaburras, like all kingfishers, are hole-nesters. They are capable of digging their own holes in a wide variety of objects providing the material is soft enough. Records show that besides trees and termite mounds, such bizarre objects as hay bales, a hole in a city building, or the large thick letters of a sign made of styrofoam may be chosen as a nest. But the award for the most unusual nesting place goes to the kookaburra who chose to lay her eggs in the ash box of an operating forge.

In my study area, kookaburras nested only in Mountain Grey Gums probably because these were the only trees large enough to support the sizeable cavity which these birds require. Generally a nest cavity has at least a five-inch diameter hole that opens directly to a chamber measuring some twelve inches in one direction with a domed roof at least nine inches high. No nest material is used; eggs are laid directly on the dust and chips naturally found on the floor of the cavity. In front of each hole at a distance of not more than twenty to thirty feet away is a perch which serves as a launching point for entering the nest. To distinguish this from other perches we called it the *perch tree*. Since the birds always alighted there before entering and after leaving the nest, it was a great centre of activity during the breeding season. This is where the vocalizations

The author shows an egg extracted from this nest hole used by two kookaburras over two consecutive years.

took place which signalled changes in nest attentiveness or the arrival of food for the chicks. As stated, most of the copulations observed were on the perch tree and during nest-showing ceremonies one bird always waited for its mate there.

Oddly enough, most nest sites were near a territorial boundary. But there may be a good reason for this. Nest-showing ceremonies occur during or after the peak in territorial adjustment around August. If a new hole must be found, there may be a higher probability that one located near a boundary would be selected rather than one in the centre of the territory simply because the birds frequent these peripheral areas more often during this busy time. These sites were not the only ones available to the birds. Often equally good holes in the middle of a territory were left untouched in preference to one near a boundary.

Kookaburra eggs are about the same size as those of a bantam's. Probably because they are laid in the safety of a hole, concealed from a predatory eye, the eggs need not be disguised by protective colouration and are therefore pure white. The clutch size can vary from one to five eggs, but two to four is the usual number. Though we haven't enough data yet, it appears that families may lay slightly larger clutches than pairs. This may be simply because egg-laying females in family groups are older and more experienced than females of pairs who, by comparison, are the newly-weds. Sometimes two clutches may be laid in a season but this only occurs in families where auxiliaries can take over the care of the first brood while the parents re-nest.

With few exceptions, eggs are laid a day apart. Since they are incubated from the moment of laying, hatching is asynchronous with the chicks appearing a day apart in the order they were laid. The incubation period ranges from twenty-four to twenty-six days.

In family groups all members actually develop a brood patch and share in incubation, auxiliaries contributing from 5% to 32% of the time observed. In some cases, this was more than the time spent by one of the breeding pair. With up to six birds taking turns on the nest, we expected to find some orderly pattern in the changing of the guard. But after hours of sitting near nests and recording the changes in attentiveness, we found no set pattern at all. We did note, however, that one of the mated pair tended to spend more time on the nest than any other member and that this same bird dominated the incubation schedule each year. For example, the breeding female of one group was the primary incubator, and in another group it was the breeding male. The primary incubator sat on the nest longer and was involved in more changes in attentiveness than other members of the family. In other words, this bird most frequently entered the nest when it was vacant and most often initiated vocalization when relieving or being relieved by another bird.

Changes in attentiveness usually proceeded in this order. A bird arrived

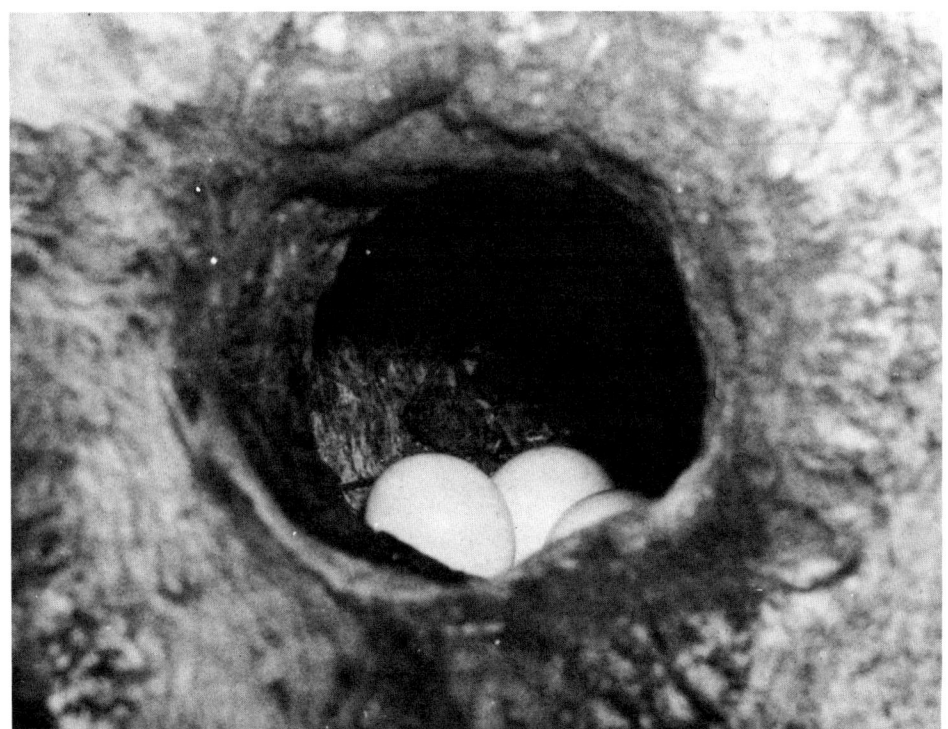

Eggs in the nest.
Newly hatched chicks with unhatched eggs in the nest.

on the perch tree and gave a soft *kooaa* followed by a *chuckle* or *chuck*. The sitting bird then came forward on the nest so it could be seen, responded with a similar call, then flew out and the relieving bird entered. But if the primary incubator was involved, the pattern was sometimes different. If she was sitting on the nest and another bird vocalized its intention to go on, she would respond but sometimes would not leave the nest. In this case the relieving bird would give up and try again later. But if the primary incubator wanted to sit and the bird already on the nest would not leave, she would simply go on the nest too. Both birds would sit together for up to five minutes until the relieved bird left.

Although we found no orderly pattern to changes of the guard, the birds from all groups averaged one and a half changes per hour with little variation. This uniformity is remarkable considering that these observations came from groups of two to six incubating individuals. It is likely that this constancy is maintained through the primary incubator. My general feeling is that this dominant individual 'lets' the others sit while he or she leaves for a quick meal or some other personal duty. Certainly auxiliaries attempted to relieve the primary incubator more often than they were allowed, and when they did sit the primary incubator rarely let the session be longer than ten minutes or so. It appears then, that although auxiliaries had a strong tendency to incubate, this was suppressed through the dominant position held by the primary incubator. Here is another instance in which the dominance hierarchy in the family group works to keep auxiliaries in check, so there is no danger of the pair's breeding rights being usurped.

The Chicks and Fledglings

In typical kingfisher fashion, kookaburra chicks are naked and blind when they hatch and they develop directly into juvenile plumage. The proverbial ugly duckling would find himself a very handsome bird in comparison with these grotesque little creatures, for kookaburra chicks have far too much skin for their small twenty-eight-gram bodies. Their wings are nothing but crooked stumps and are all out of proportion with their large feet and legs. A close look at the structure above the neck shows that the three lobes of almost equal size are actually two unopened eyes and a skull. Between these gigantic eye orbs is perched a tiny but wide blackish-coloured beak. This is tipped with a small white hook or egg tooth, a device which the young bird uses like a can opener to effect its escape from the shell.

After hatching, the chicks avoid the perilous fall out of the nest partially by use of their remarkable sense of touch. First they huddle against unhatched eggs and then against the back wall of the chamber. I suspect that they can also

Two young kookaburras over 10 days old. (Frauca)

Three older chicks showing the effects of asynchronous hatching.

perceive light through their unopened lids, for they were always turned away from the nest entrance whenever I looked in.

Kookaburra chicks grow slowly for a bird and it takes from twenty-seven to thirty-three days before full plumage is attained. In this time the chicks go from one form of ugliness to another as various stages in their development proceed.

Days Old	Stage of Development	Weight in Grams
1 – 7	completely naked and blind	28
7 –11	pins on body and wings emerge	81
7 –13	slits form on eyelids	81
10–13	eyelids begin to open	134
10–15	pins grow and show pigmentation	134
14–17	eyelids fully opened	196
17–22	pin shafts on body and wing split	245
22–27	pin shafts on head and flight feathers split	285
27–33	pin shafts around face split, bird fully plumed	300
33–39	bird remains in nest before fledging	313

mean adult weight = 353 grams
mean weight of chicks at fledging = 330 grams

Like the young of other hole-nesters, fledgling kookaburras can fly well upon leaving the nest, a feat not common among birds that nest in the open. It seems that the extra time spent in the nest may be necessary to build up strength for this first flight and this probably accounts for the comparatively long nestling phase seen in the kookaburra and other hole-nesting species.

We noted previously that kookaburras hatched asynchronously. This means that in a clutch of four eggs, the first to hatch would be four days old by the time the last chick emerges. It is not hard to see how this could function as a natural regulating device if food was scarce. The youngest in the nest, having the weakest food-begging cry would be first to die, leaving the older and stronger individuals to share the limited food. By contrast, in good seasons where all the young could be fed, there is no risk of the stronger ones jeopardising the survival of their weaker nest mates.

This principle may have been operating in the population I studied. There was a major outbreak of Cicadas during the 1966 breeding season and the kookaburras stuffed their young with so many of these insects that often the young would turn away, so full that they just could not take another. There is no doubt that this would be considered a good season, far better than the average conditions met in the 1965 breeding season. Now, let us look at the effect that asynchronous hatching had on the young of these two different

Above: *Half-plumed chick.*
Below: *Chick with pin feathers developing.*

years. In 1965, seven nests were observed. In three of these, the youngest chick died, two within a week after hatching. In 1966, the year of the food glut, I knew the initial brood size of eleven of the fourteen nests watched and only one youngest chick died. In addition, this was the only year in which a clutch of four eggs all hatched and here too even the runt of the family survived.

One interesting little field experiment gave us further insight into this matter. A solitary pair had three chicks in a nest low enough to be reached with a step ladder. I marked the chicks according to their age so each could be recognized at a glance. Then I laid out cubes of meat for the parents to deliver to the hungry mouths. Every time a parent fed a chick I would dash up the ladder in time to see which was the lucky receiver. After about twenty repetitions of this I tallied up the score and found that the eldest was repeatedly fed first by both adults. After some six cubes the second eldest was fed. The youngest was always the last to receive a morsel. Obviously the chick sitting most forward in the nest would be most likely to be fed first, but in this case the youngest sat most forward and still was not favoured.

Although this data looks conclusive, I tested the chicks' growth rates to see if youngest chicks had lower weight gain than their older nest mates. On account of the difference in food abundance, I also tested to see if 1966 chicks gained weight faster than the 1965 chicks. As the answer to both tests was negative, it must be assumed that the observed deaths of youngest chicks could have occurred by chance. So what is needed now is more data covering many more years of fluctuating food supplies. Perhaps the food resources in my study area were never low enough to really jeopardise the runts' chances of survival. All we can say at present is that it appears that asynchronous hatching has some effect on survival but the importance of this has yet to be found.

Small and helpless though they appear, kookaburra chicks have quite a range of behaviour. They maintain their own nest sanitation by turning their posterior to the nest hole and ejecting a liquid excretia. Believe it or not, a man named Thomson took measurements of this and found that kookaburra chicks forced their excreta a distance of some thirty-two inches, far enough to reach the outside without fouling the hole or cavity.[22] It is interesting to recall how the parents remodel the nest chamber so that it lies in line with the hole and thus facilitates the efficiency of this voiding behaviour. I was grateful for this clever adaptation because it certainly made my nest investigations more pleasant than they could have been.

Some authors maintain that hole-nesting chicks perceive light through their unopened lids and that the stimulus to gape for food is triggered by the darkening of the hole as the adult passes through. This is not true for kookaburras, however. The stimulus to raise that wobbly head and thrust open the little beak is triggered by the soft *chucks* and *chuckles* of the adult. I first suspected this when I heard five-day-old chicks cheeping in response to a food-bearing bird who gave the *chuck* call on the perch tree but had not yet entered the nest. This was substantiated by an observation which now stands out as the most memorable event in my bird watching career.

I had climbed a tree containing a nest of three newly-hatched young. My head was at the level of the hole and as I fumbled about trying to weigh the eldest chick, I suddenly felt the sweep of wings on my cheek. I was absolutely astonished to see that the adult female had entered the nest, considering my presence as nonchalantly as if I were but another branch. Carrying a small worm, she walked to the centre of the cavity and gently squatted down on her remaining two chicks. Feeling somewhat like a thief caught in the act, I replaced the eldest chick on the lip of the hole and hardly daring to breathe, watched the following events.

The little blind creature waddled to its mother and crawled under her breast. She, with worm still in beak, gave a short series of soft *chucks*. The youngster reappeared from beneath her breast feathers, threw its head back and gaped. The worm was crammed into the tiny orifice in what seemed a terribly rough manner, and when all but one end of the worm was tucked in, the contented chick returned to maternal warmth.

The female sat quietly for some minutes, her beak not six inches from my nose. Then she gently lifted herself off her charges and left. Not daring to press her hospitality by waiting for her return, I quickly weighed the other chicks and climbed down the ladder feeling very contented to have shared in this experience.

However their hospitality did not last long, for as the adults' instinct to care for their offspring increased, the chicks also developed the ability to protest at being handled. The result was always a confusion of dive-bombing swoops and *cackles* whenever my presence at the nest was detected. It is not easy to hang onto a rope ladder some thirty feet up, let alone try to stuff a chick into a bag and get its weight, hoping against hope that the little monster will be quiet so as not to stir up parental wrath. Invariably the chick would let out an alarming *squawk* and I immediately became a vulnerable target for the rest of the family.

Inevitably one day I was hit right at the base of my skull. I only hope the impact gave that kookaburra as big a headache as he gave me. From then on I wore a safety helmet and this solved everything but my shattered nerves. In two years of climbing to nests daily, I never got over the anxiety of being dive-bombed, nor did the kookaburras ever tire of giving me the full treatment. But I was not their only victim. Late one evening the mother of a week-old chick emerged from her hole some forty feet up to make a last search for food before the dwindling light brought her hectic day to a close. Then she discovered that looming only ten feet above her nest was a huge Greater Glider, the size of a tom cat. In a split second she was in her sleeked dive bomber's position barrelling down on this awful intruder. With one powerful thud she hit the glider's neck and it went sailing all of fifty feet out of the tree looking exactly like a flying carpet. As it hit the ground the very frightened creature couldn't gather itself fast enough to run for cover before she was on it again with a *cackle* and a crack at its neck. The glider made fast tracks up the nearest tree and disappeared into thick foliage. With her wrath satisfied, the kookaburra proceeded on her food-gathering venture.

As any parent knows, a baby's day is largely just one continuum of begging for and receiving food. Kookaburra chicks are certainly no exception. From the time the chicks hatch, auxiliaries and parents alike form into a monotonous shuttle service running between hunting ground and gaping beak. During this time solitary pairs are under considerable pressure as each bird contributes equally to feeding the chicks. Among families though, all members shouldered this duty with auxiliaries contributing between 10% and 61% of all items brought. Because of this extra help, parents in family groups had much more free time than did the solitary pairs.

The tendency to pass food from one individual to another appears to be very strong in many birds. Aviculturists know that in abnormal caged conditions, birds often engage in this behaviour and can even pass food to birds of other species. Dr Skutch, a foremost authority on extra-parental care in birds, notes that after alarm systems, 'the next most common mode of helpfulness among birds is in feeding. Since survival of most species depends upon the parents' placing sufficient food into the mouths of their young, the urge to give food to other individuals has become very strong in birds. It is one of the first forms of parental behaviour to become manifest in the young and it has been observed even in nestlings. Finally, it is one of the last modes of parental behaviour to disappear when a species becomes parasitic and depends on others to rear its progeny.'[19]

This drive is so strong in kookaburras that even an auxiliary with a badly wounded leg contributed, with great difficulty, some 14% of the items brought to the nest. Sometimes food was passed twice before being fed to the chicks. A food-bearing adult would pass its item to a brooding adult, which then passed it to the chick.

In one family group where a second clutch was laid after the first brood fledged, the fledgling of the first brood was still being fed by the auxiliaries. When the eggs hatched it wasn't long before this fledgling also attempted to feed the new chicks along with the others of the family. This fledgling would give a food begging *squawk* and when an adult passed food to it, it would go to the perch tree, give a very inexperienced version of a *chuck* or *chuckle*, bash the item, then fly to the nest and pass it to the chick inside. Though this youngster never got very good at the technique, it still contributed 10% of the items fed to this second brood of the season.

By the time a chick is thirty-three to thirty-nine days old it must leave the sanctuary of its protected hole and make its big plunge into the outside world. As in the order of laying and hatching, fledgling too is an asynchronous affair, each bird leaves the nest a day apart in order of age.

Several hours before this big step, the young bird comes forward and sits near the lip of the hole. It stretches its wings repeatedly and pecks at the bark around the hole as if biding its time. One or two adults may sit on the perch tree and seem to try and lure the youngster out by giving *chucks* and *chuckles*. Once I saw the parents fetch food and bring it to the perch tree. Upon seeing these tasty morsels, the chick piped up with a begging *squawk*. But the parents just sat with the food for several minutes and then, right in front of their hungry offspring, they tossed their heads back and ate the food themselves. This seemed to do the trick, for in the next instance the youngster was out of the nest making a bee-line for the ground some fifty feet away. In the four fledging events I saw, the manner of leaving the nest was the same; other than coaxing from a distance, adults did not help in any way.

When the bird lit on the ground, the adults flew to it, and after excited rounds of laughter, the fledgling flew to a low perch in a dense bush where it remained quietly for the remainder of the day. The fledglings never returned to the nest, nor were they taken to the roosting site. They were left in thick foliage at dusk and were visited again at the crack of dawn. The day after a bird fledged, the adults would lead it away from the nest area to some spot with a thick cover of foliage. Among families, one bird usually sat with the fledglings but among pairs, the fledglings were often found sitting alone.

Fledglings are totally dependent on adults for food for about eight weeks. Anyone living near a group of fledgling kookaburras will admit that putting up with the harsh grating din of their ceaseless food-begging calls is enough to try the patience of Job.

For the first two to three weeks, fledglings stay within the same thickly-foliated area. Here they spend their time preening, sun bathing, sparring with vegetation and practising their very clumsy landings by making short flights from tree to tree until they finally learn to land without using their beaks as a prop. Adults seem to encourage these flying lessons by landing away from the fledglings and giving the feeding vocalizations so that the young birds must fly to the adult to be fed.

Over the weeks, fledglings become more agile and begin to fly with the adults, watching the daily routine and eventually joining in such activities as laughing in chorus, giving trapeze displays and sleeping with the family on the communal roosting perch.

Around mid-December or early January adults begin to moult and their tendency to feed their young noticeably decreases. At this time the fledglings have been out of the nest for some eight to thirteen weeks. At first, adults seem to pass food reluctantly but as body moult progresses there is a noticeable difference in their behaviour for they become very anti-social. If a fledgling lands next to a heavily-moulting adult and begs for food, the adult usually responds with a belting that often knocks the youngster right off the perch. Experiences like these soon teach the fledgling that its pampered days are over and it must now consider itself independent. But for some weeks before adults finally 'break the plate', the youngsters do attempt to feed themselves. This is a very vulnerable time for them however, because they are so inexperienced. They stay on the ground for perilously long periods, unaware that predators like foxes and cats may be lurking behind the bushes. Thus, it is not surprising to find that heavy mortality occurs during this period.

The hormones responsible for the start of moult are coupled with the reproductive hormones; one wanes as the other waxes. Because the breeding urge of auxiliaries is suppressed, they start to moult before their parents, the younger ones usually starting before the older ones. The breeding pair start at the same time but they are the last of the family to do so.

Feather replacement follows in this order; tail, body, head and wings, flight feathers. It is only during body moult that the birds are very anti-social. The whole process takes about three months, but often younger auxiliaries have almost completed their heavy body moult before the parents begin the first process of replacing their tail feathers. This phenomenon of staggered moult may have an interesting repercussion on the survival of the fledglings. Among pairs, fledgling independence is forced irrevocably when the parents begin to moult because they start to do so at the same time. In families, however, auxiliaries that had finished body moult were seen to resume passing food to fledglings even though the parents had ceased feeding them altogether. Thus, among families the period of parental care was extended in some cases up to five weeks beyond that received by young of pairs. We will discuss the implications of this when we compare the overall breeding success of pairs and families.

The whole breeding process, from the time eggs are laid to the time of fledgling independence, takes fifteen to nineteen weeks. This is an incredibly long time considering that food must be gathered throughout this period. For this reason, it is improbable that a single pair could successfully rear a second brood after the first had been raised to independence. Even if their nest was plundered late in the season, their chances of successfully making a second attempt would be low. But in families, auxiliaries can and do take over the care and feeding of the first fledglings, which leaves the breeding female free to nest again. Of course, environmental conditions must be good to ensure

Nearly-plumed chick.

that food will still be plentiful for the second lot of youngsters. Probably as a result of the glut of Cicadas in 1966, two families in my study area laid a second clutch of eggs. The clutches, each of three eggs, were started on 7 November and 26 November. One egg from each hatched on 7 December and 22 December respectively. One chick was missing two days after hatching but the other fledged on the 10 January.

There is an unusual observation to relate about the laying of one of these two second clutches. It was a particularly sunny day and I cheerfully took to the bush with the prospect of watching the fledging of the only chick in Aunt Clara's family. Sure enough, I arrived in the nest area to find the little fellow sitting forward in the entrance watching the coaxing antics of Aunt Clara and Young Green (her auxiliary brother hatched in 1965). Finally, at 12.30 p.m. the fledgling made the big plunge and started his life in the real world. This was something of a nostalgic event for me for it marked the end of many pleasant and painful hours of watching that nest. But just as I was about to leave, strange things began to happen.

Young Gold (Young Green's nest mate from 1965), arrived on the perch tree with a lizard. After a bash and a *chuckle* he flew to the nest but finding it empty, flew off to enjoy the morsel himself. Right after this, the breeding female came to the perch tree and began to give a most peculiar *soft squawk*, the courtship call I hadn't heard for over two months. She anxiously pranced to and fro on the perch and finally, at 1.00 p.m., she went into the nest. In a burst of activity she kicked and scratched at the floor of the cavity until showers of dirt and debris came pouring out of the hole. My first thought was that someone had delivered a live snake to the nest and she was desperately battling to kill it. Minutes later she came out looking a bit worn but still very anxious. The breeding male greeted her on the perch tree but when she again gave *soft squawks* he just gave her a puzzled look. Both then left the area but returned at 1.30 p.m. In the meantime I climbed to the nest just to check on my snake idea. It was empty but the cavity looked very clean. When the female returned, she entered the hole and again thrashed the floor violently, causing more refuse to shower out. On her return to the perch tree, the male flew to the nest and he too began to thrash dirt out of the hole. At 2.00 p.m. both left and shortly the female returned, her mate close behind bearing a lizard. She gave one anxious *soft squawk* on the perch tree and he passed the morsel to her.

When the area was again cleared, I climbed to the nest for another check and saw that it was still empty. With this as my only understandable fact, I sat to wait for the next event in this bizarre day. At 3.00 p.m. the female again entered the hole, this time quietly. In about ten minutes I could see her make movements that looked as if she was preening her tail and a few moments later she quietly left the nest. Sure enough, when I scurried up the tree I found a new, warm, white egg in the same depression that just two and half hours before had contained a chick.

Looking back on the events of these two-and-a-half hours was like watching a sped-up movie film of the whole courtship sequence with all the comical hysteria that fast action brings. This is, of course, was exactly what happened. Apparently in order to lay an egg, the pair must go through the whole sequence of stereotyped courtship behaviour, even though it must be done in two and a half hours instead of four weeks. Goodness knows what would have happened had the fledgling been a bit slow in leaving the nest . . .

8. MORTALITY AND PREDATION

Mortality can occur at any stage in a kookaburra's life cycle but as is usual in the animal world, death takes its highest toll in the first year of life. Of the fifty-one eggs laid in both years of the study, eighteen failed to hatch. Of these, three contained dead embryos, ten were infertile and five were snatched by predators, leaving an overall hatching success of 66%. By comparison on a world wide basis, Mrs Nice and other researchers have recorded a 75% success for twelve hole-nesting species and 62% for open-nesting species.[24]

Six chicks died before fledging and as stated previously, four of these were the youngest of the brood. While only one chick definitely died of starvation, the other three probably succumbed to the same fate. At least they could not have been victims of predation because their nest mates were left unharmed. However, two other chicks most likely did become meals for predators. Each was the only chick in the brood and their weights had been normal the day before they were missing. In both these cases the nests also contained unhatched eggs and they too had been taken. So, of our original number of eggs, only 50% of them produced birds of fledgling age. This is again lower than the 65% recorded for other hole-nesters but slightly higher than the 48% recorded for open nesters.[24]

Just who these elusive predators were was a bit of a mystery, since we never caught a culprit in the act. But with a bit of detective work we were able to narrow the field to three suspects. In one case, we checked a clutch of two eggs at the end of the day and returned early next morning to find nothing but empty shells that were still sticky on the insides. The carnivorous Brush-tailed Phascogale, commonly found in our area, licks the contents of eggs in this manner, and since he also has an appetite for young nestlings, I feel sure we can attribute to him some of our losses. This rat-sized marsupial lives in hollow tree-branches where he would have easy access to other animals' nest-holes.

Some mammalogists are convinced that possums and gliders are vegetarians and therefore have no interest in eggs or nestlings. But other workers have found eggshells in possums' stomachs and insist that the odd egg, and probably nestling too, does form a small part of their diet. Possums so frequently took over kookaburra nest holes for sleeping quarters that they probably knew where to go for a quick meal. Also, from the wrath displayed by a breeding female toward a Greater Glider, one naturally suspects that it, or something like it, is a recognized predator. In those cases where eggs disappeared altogether, I suspect some of our furry phalangers were at work.

Keith Hindwood has observed a Grey Butcher Bird 'tearing apart a nestling kookaburra it had removed from a nearby hollow.'[6] One of the chicks of a second brood of the season mysteriously disappeared from its hole which, by coincidence, was very near a Butcher Bird's nest.

Fledgling kookaburras suffer little mortality when they leave the nest because they receive so much parental care. When they learn to feed on their own, however, they probably fill the stomachs of a few cats and foxes. More than once I've had to distract a cat who was ready to pounce on a preoccupied young kookaburra and by the same token, I've picked up three carcasses of tagged fledglings which had been dismembered by some terrestrial predator.

Juvenile mortality is particularly heavy in kookaburras within the first few months after their newly-attained independence. Of the twenty-two eggs laid in 1965, thirteen produced young who became independent and of these, only six were alive the following September. Most of these birds disappeared before June, and though I found only three carcasses, I am sure the others could not have dispersed from the area. They too probably died.

Those kookaburras who do make it through the first year seem to have a high survival rate. One old kookaburra in the study area was known to a reliable observer by a small plumage deformity. He was breeding when this observer first met him, and ten years later he was still the father of young. The C.S.I.R.O. Bird Banding Scheme produced a record of a kookaburra who was recaptured six years after the band was first put on. I returned to my old study area over the 1968 Christmas holidays and although there were some new faces I was delighted to find most of my old tagged kookaburras still there, including Aunt Clara who was still a spinster in her parents' territory. At any rate, birds who were adult when I met them early in 1965 were still active and healthy nearly four years later.

Longevity records are difficult to assess in nature, but we do know that bigger birds tend to have a longer life span than smaller birds. Even with this knowledge, kookaburras seem to have a surprisingly long life.

9. WHY HAVE AUXILIARIES?

As you will remember, the basic aim of our enquiry into the kookaburra's breeding biology was to find out what advantages family groups had over solitary pairs. If young of families have a higher survival rate over the young of pairs, we will know the adaptive significance of the auxiliary social system.

We mentioned that for a species to continue, its members must survive long enough to leave offspring, and those offspring in turn must be fit enough to reproduce. Since kookaburras are capable of reproducing at the age of twelve months, we must consider survival in all age classes from egg-laying to one year old. While we have such data for 1965, the study ended in May 1967 before a full assessment of the 1966 success was known. But even so, our results are impressive. In 1965 the total mortality from egg to one year old was 40% among families while among pairs it was 100%. For 1966 the figure was tending toward the same result, even though our tally only goes up to the young juvenile stage. As it was, in 1966, the mortality among families was only 22%, whereas among pairs it was already 50%. So it certainly appears that natural selection favours family groups with auxiliaries. It is likely that once a solitary pair manages to rear a chick which survives its first year, that bird would remain with its parents as an auxiliary. Having thus attained family status, the pairs' chances of success in future breeding attempts would be greatly enhanced.

But just how does the presence of auxiliaries increase the survival chances of the family? The most obvious hypothesis is that since families have larger territories in which to gather food, and more members to bring that food to the nest, their young should be healthier than those from pairs. To test this, I compared the growth rates of chicks raised by pairs with those raised by families for both years. It was startling to find that there was no difference as both grew equally well.

This result was so unexpected that I tackled the matter from another approach. By sitting with a good view of the perch tree, I could count the number of feeding visits each adult made to the nest in any one day. With a pair of binoculars, I could even see what items were being brought. First I

Three young fledglings.

compared the size of the items brought with the ages of the chicks and found that both pairs and families fed their young the same general menu and that the size of the morsel increased with the age of the chicks. Knowing this, I could now test to see if three or more adults brought more food (i.e., made more feeding visits) than did two birds. There was no relationship at all, indicating that the number of feeding visits made by pairs and families was nearly the same. I may have guessed the answer even before this test because the average number of visits per thirty minutes was 1.7 for pairs and 1.5 for families.

Our basic hypothesis is therefore wrong. Having bigger territories and more helpers does not mean that the young are better fed. This may not be too surprising, however, if the amount of food brought to the nest is not a critical factor in determining future survival. It may be that spring's bounty offers plenty of food for all the birds regardless of the size of the hunting ground or the number of birds bringing the food.

As noted before, mortality started to become heavy as the fledglings became independent. This event occurs around January when food may not be as abundant as it was in springtime. This shortage would have a greater impact if the hunter was an inexperienced kookaburra forced to suddenly fend for itself. If, however, there was even just one adult capable of helping to make this transition easier by extending the period of parental care, young kookaburras may find their survival chances somewhat enhanced. This appears to be the case in family groups where moult is staggered and the parental care period can be extended.

Auxiliary assistance most directly benefits the breeding pair. With auxiliaries taking a share in incubation of eggs and feeding of young, the breeding pair has much more free time to devote to their own welfare, a luxury not afforded to solitary pairs. Subjectively speaking, parents with helpers certainly looked less stressed than those without help. And as mentioned before, in a good food year, breeding females of families can spend their spare time gathering enough nourishment to form eggs for a second clutch. With auxiliaries to take over the care of the first brood, the pair can devote time and energy to rearing the second brood. (Auxiliaries were seen to help with the second brood also, but only after the young of the first brood were nearly independent.)

And what of the auxiliaries? Do they benefit in any way from all of this? It appears that there are two courses a kookaburra can take when it is a year or more old. It can leave its parents' territory during the dispersal period in July and August and become a vagrant, seeking unclaimed territory. However, from the injury rate among vagrants and their very small proportion in the population, this course seems to be a very risky one. Perhaps older auxiliaries, whose urge to breed is too great for them to remain subordinate to their parents, take this opportunity as a last ditch measure. They either successfully establish themselves or they die.

The second alternative for a sexually mature auxiliary is to abide within the sanctuary of its parents' territory until one of its parents or a breeding neighbour dies. The auxiliary then simply moves over and fills the vacancy. This happened three times in this two-year study. While living in its parents' territory, the auxiliary may gain valuable experience in the art of defending a territory and rearing a brood which may be useful to its own survival when it becomes a breeder itself.

Now that we have ascertained the survival value of the auxiliary system, we could end our story here. But there is one more puzzling question which deserves attention. A combined census of the study area taken just before the breeding season showed that there were nineteen pairs and twenty-five auxiliaries in residence. Yet, an examination of our breeding figures shows us that families with two or more auxiliaries were no more successful than those with only one helper. Why then do we find so many auxiliaries? The sex ratio of the population was balanced so we cannot propose that over one third of the adult population did not breed because they were members of the excess sex.

The answer may well be linked with the way this species regulates its numbers to prevent over-population. Perhaps because of man's growing concern over his own population problems, this field of ecology has just recently come under careful scrutiny. Many researchers are gathering data from animals in nature. The fruits of these studies are yielding so much information that there is now a wide range of interesting theories to consider. To find which theory best fits the kookaburra, we will confine our attention to two possibilities. These revolve around whether or not this species is reproducing at a maximum rate or at an optimum rate.

When we watch some populations grow in the laboratory, we see that given a favourable environment, the numbers usually increase rapidly until some resource necessary for survival becomes limiting. Then individuals start to compete for the limited resource and the weaker individuals, less successful in competition, are eliminated either through starvation, predation, disease or other factors. The birth rate tends to remain constant, so as more and more pressure is applied to the limited resource, more and more individuals compete for it and die. This death rate, being density dependent, is the prime regulator of the population. Since this rate is ultimately determined by the maximum birth rate, we can call this the Maximal Reproductive Rate Theory.

Dr David Lack's field studies on many different bird species support these laboratory observations which indicate that natural selection does tend to favour a maximum reproductive output and that populations in nature do regulate through density dependent mortality. According to this view, all the optimum breeding spaces are filled with the most efficient breeders who rear as many young as they can successfully feed.[7,8]

But not all birds conform to the Maximal Reproductive Rate Theory. Whereas Dr Lack's data comes largely from Northern Hemisphere birds, Dr Alexander Skutch has spent his life in Central America studying tropical birds. He finds that in many cases reproduction is not at its maximum rate; parents could successfully rear more young than they do. This is especially true in those species where the female single-handedly rears the brood and manages to rear as many young as do those species where the pair co-operate in this duty. Dr Skutch also notes that birds tend to live longer in the tropics than do those living in the more northern latitudes where harsh winters and perilous migrations trim longevity to a minimum. From these observations, Dr Skutch returns to an earlier view and asks if animals could be reproducing only as fast as they must to keep up with the death rate. In other words, the birth rate, not the death rate is density dependent. This is referred to as the Optimal Reproductive Rate Theory.[20]

Though some researchers disagree, Dr Skutch argues that these two theories are simply extremes of the same scale. In milder climates where there are few limiting factors in the environment, death rate is naturally low and to avoid over populating, animals must reproduce at a correspondingly lower rate. But colder climates impose so many limiting factors on the population that the death rate is naturally higher and in many cases animals must reproduce at maximum rate to keep up with it.

If we agree with Dr Skutch that natural selection determines the birth rate in accordance with the death rate, we can see that in cold climates special adaptations have been selected to yield a maximum output, but in warmer climates other adaptations have been favoured which keep the birth rate optimum.

The question now is whether or not the kookaburra's auxiliary system is an adaptation for keeping the birth rate low. Two lines of evidence show us that this may be the case. First, kookaburras are long-lived birds. They may owe their longevity to the fact that they are living in one of the milder climates of the world. They are naturally distributed along the wetter portions of Australia's east coast where the climate is seldom severe enough to cause great mortality. Kookaburras' broad food preferences and apparent ability to subsist without free water may also contribute to their longevity.

The second piece of evidence is seen in the delayed reproduction of the auxiliaries. On the one hand, we have shown that this delayed reproduction has survival value because family groups rear young more successfully than do solitary pairs. But on the other hand, these auxiliaries are forming about one third of the adult population and by not breeding, they may be effectively lowering the birth rate in accordance with the population's lowered death rate.

Proponents of the Maximal Reproductive Rate Theory, however, would argue that auxiliaries are necessary for the survival of the species, for as we

Kookaburra peers out of its nesting burrow excavated on a termitarium up a tree. (Frauca)

have seen, solitary pairs are not very successful breeders. Therefore, perhaps kookaburras are reproducing as fast as they can after all, and auxiliaries are necessary for this maximum output. This is certainly true to an extent. The presence of one auxiliary does enhance the group's survival, but our data shows that the presence of two or more auxiliaries in a family is no more beneficial than having only one. In some territories there were as many as four auxiliaries and I've seen groups that had many more. The presence of three- and four-year-old non-breeding adults is evidence that kookaburras are not reproducing as fast as they could if all these older auxiliaries were breeding.

Then too, we must not forget the implications of territorial behaviour in this argument. Auxiliaries must occupy as much space as do their breeding parents so that the parents' resources are not robbed. We know that possession of a territory is a requisite for breeding and yet we find that these prime spaces are filled by non-breeding birds. We certainly would not expect this to occur if kookaburras were breeding as fast as they could. As it is, territorial behaviour insures that the birth rate is kept below maximum.

Kookaburras then, seem to have evolved the auxiliary social system because of its survival value and by doing so, they have insured against over-population by curbing their birth rate to equal their low death rate. We must remember that regulation on this scale is a long term adaptation, one that affects the population as a whole over a broad period of time. But the selection of this social system as an adaptation to maintain an optimal reproductive rate does not mean that density dependent mortality is a negligible factor. What happens when there are fluctuations between good and bad food years? Looking at this matter on a short term basis as we have done in this study, we see that in a good food year, families lay double clutches and in a poor year, there are losses among the surplus young. These are surely density dependent fluctuations which are necessary to keep the immediate population in tune with its surroundings. In other words, even with sociality operating to curb the potential birth rate, density dependent mortality influences the immediate population. But, by being density dependent, this mortality does not operate at the same rate in all years, and like the opportunity to lay double clutches, may be a short term adaptation by which annual adjustments to the population balance are made.

Our story of the kookaburra started with one simple question. How does this bird live? Over the course of these pages we have followed the kookaburra's life cycle and made many unexpected and fascinating discoveries. But, as is typical in most fields of research, we must end our story with another more complex question. How does this species regulate its numbers? So far we

Why Have Auxiliaries? 105

have only lifted the lid enough to reveal some evidence which allows us to set up an hypothesis. Now our research must start anew with this more complex question as the aim of our inquiry. No one knows yet how many more questions will require answers before we can finally draw the story to a close.

But this preliminary study has done more than just stir up more perplexing questions. We have made an important probe into the little-understood phenomena of sociality. We have clearly seen how a social system very similar to our own is of definite survival value in another species. Kookaburras have adopted the social way of life so fully that it is manifested in almost every aspect of their lives. For instance, uniform plumage characters and a repertoire of simple communal vocalizations insure that the system runs efficiently.

In visual behaviour we see a minimum of patterns performed by the individual alone. Those performed solely by the pair were simple courtship patterns designed to isolate the pair from the group, reinforce the bond and attach the pair to a nest site. The remainder of the patterns involved the group as a whole and these centred on the reinforcement of the family hierarchy and the maintenance of territory.

We saw how the hierarchy was the basis of the social system as it suppressed the breeding urge of the auxiliaries and kept them subordinate to the breeding pair.

As a diversion into various aspects of territorial behaviour, we saw first how territorial displays evolved, then how they functioned to keep the group exclusive and confined to one area the year round. Their strong drive to maintain territory also helped to cement the family bond.

Then too, we saw that each adult bird required a certain amount of space to live in and that this size was probably determined behaviourally by the amount of space the birds could successfully defend. The territorial requirements of non-breeding auxiliaries were the same as those of the breeding pair and so territorial behaviour also functions to keep the birth rate of the population below that expected if only breeding birds were allowed to hold territories.

The importance of the auxiliary social system came to the fore when we studied the kookaburra's breeding biology. By comparing their success with solitary pairs, we saw that families were far more successful in rearing young. However, the full co-operation the auxiliaries gave to incubating eggs and feeding young did not seem to account for this differential success. But when the young started to become independent, we did note that those from families fared better probably because the staggered moult in the parents and non-breeders extended the period of parental care. The presence of auxiliaries not only enhanced the survival chances of the young but allowed the parents more free time away from nesting duties which in turn allowed them to re-nest if the environment was favourable. Auxiliaries too, benefit from this system, for those who eventually become breeders are likely to survive better as a result of the experience gained while in the sanctuary of their parents' territory.

On close examination of the system as a whole, we noted that auxiliaries constituted over one third of the adult population and that two or more auxiliaries contributed no more to a family's breeding success than did one auxiliary. From this, sociality seems to have another function apart from its survival value alone. Kookaburras are long-lived birds probably because they live along Australia's east coast where the climate is mild. In accordance with the Optimal Reproductive Rate Theory, special adaptations may have been selected to keep the birth rate in tune with the population's low death rate. Though this hypothesis requires further testing, it appears that the auxiliary social system may be one such special adaptation.

If nothing else, the reality of this unusual system in the kookaburra increases our knowledge of the great number of animals who have evolved strange and often wondrous mechanisms for adapting to our unique island continent.

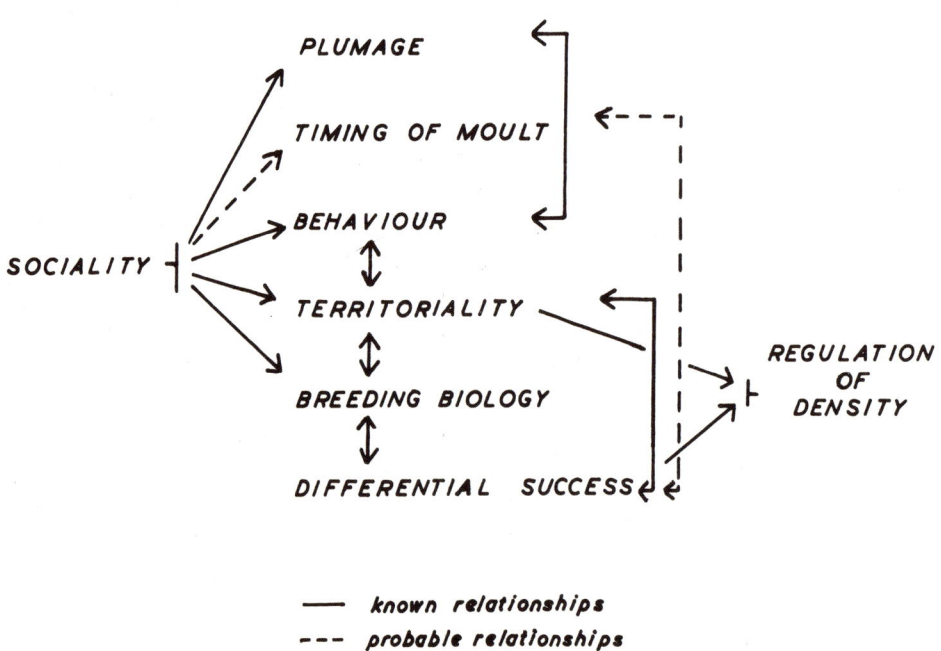

Diagram showing possible and known relationships between sociality and regulation of population density.

LIST OF SCIENTIFIC NAMES

Apostle-bird *Struthidea cinerea*
Babblers *Pomatostomus* spp.
Brush-tailed Phascogale *Phascogale tapoafota*
Cicada *Cyclochila australasiae*
Eastern Rosella *Platycercus eximius*
Greater Glider *Schonobates volans*
Grey Butcher Bird *Cracticus torquatus*
Magpie *Gymnorhina tibicen*
Maned Goose (Wood-Duck) *Chenonetta jubata*
Mexican Brown Jay *Psilorhinus mexicanus*
Mountain Grey Gum *Eucalyptus cypellocarpa*
Pied Butcher Bird *Cracticus nigrogularis*
Possum *Pseudocheirus* spp.
Powerful Owl *Ninox strenua*
Superb Blue Wren *Malurus cyaneus*
Tasmanian Native Hen *Tribonyx mortierii*
Wedge-tailed Eagle *Aquila audax*
White-winged Chough *Corcorax melanorhamphus*

BIBLIOGRAPHY

1. A.J.C. 'Forgotten Feathers', *Emu* **7**, pp. 193–196, 1908.
2. Alexander, W. B., 'Sonnerat's Voyage to New Guinea', *Emu* **23**, pp. 299–305, 1924.
3. Brereton, J. Le Gay, 'Inter-animal Control of Space: The Role of Rank Order, Parent-Offspring Relations, and Peer Play. Illustrated by Comparative Studies of Australian Parrots', *The Use of Space by Animals and Men*, edited by A. H. Esser, Indiana University Press, 1969.
4. Caley, George, *Reflections on the Colony of New South Wales*, edited by J. Currey, Lansdowne Press, Melbourne 1966.
5. Harrison, C. J. O., 'Helpers at the Nest in Australian Passerine Birds', *Emu* **69**, pp. 30–40, 1969.
6. Hindwood, K. A., 'Nesting Habits of the Kookaburra or Laughing Jackass (*Dacelo gigas*)', *Emu* **47**, pp. 117–130, 1947.
7. Lack, D., *Population Studies of Birds*, Clarendon Press, 1966.
8. Lack, D., *Ecological Adaptations for Breeding in Birds*, Methuen & Co., London 1968.
9. Leach, J. A., 'The Naming of Australian Birds', *Emu* **24**, pp. 170–182, 1925.
10. Lysaght, A., 'Why did Sonnerat Record the Kookaburra *Dacelo gigas* (Boddaert) from New Guinea?', *Emu* **56**, pp. 224–225, 1956.
11. Matthews, G. M., 'Correspondence to the Editor', *Emu* **26**, p. 148, 1926.
12. Morris, E. E., *Austral English: A Dictionary of Australian Words, Phrases and Usages*, Macmillan, London 1898.
13. RAOU Checklist Committee, *Official Checklist of the Birds of Australia*, 2nd ed., Government Printer, Melbourne 1926.
14. R.A.O.U. Report, 'R.A.O.U. Annual Congress and Campout', *Emu* **22**, pp. 199–205, 1923.
15. Ridpath, M. G., 'The Tasmanian Native Hen', *Aust. Nat. Hist.*, **14** (11), pp. 346–350, 1964.
16. Rowley, I., 'The Life History of the Superb Blue Wren, *Malurus cyaneis*', *Emu* **64**, pp. 251–297, 1965.

17. Rowley, I., 'White Winged Choughs', *Aust. Nat. Hist.*, **15**(3), pp. 81–85, 1965.
18. Rowley, I., 'Communal Species of Australian Birds', *Bonner Zoologische Beittrage*, **3**/**4**, pp. 362–368, 1968.
19. Skutch, A. F., 'Helpers Among Birds', *Condor* **63**, pp. 198–226, 1961.
20. Skutch, A. F., 'Adaptive Limitation of the Reproductive Rate of Birds', *Ibis* **109**, pp. 579–599, 1967.
21. Sonnerat, Pierre, *Voyage a la Nouville Guinnee*, p. 171, Paris, 1776.
22. Thomson, D. F., 'Some Adaptations for the Disposal of Faeces. The Hygiene of the Nest in Australian Birds', *Proc. Zool. Soc. London*, pp. 701–707, 1934–5.
23. von Haartman, L., 'Adaptations in Hole-nesting Birds', *Evol.* **11**(2), pp. 339–347, 1957.
24. Welty, J. C., *The Life of Birds*. W. B. Saunders Co., Philadelphia 1962.